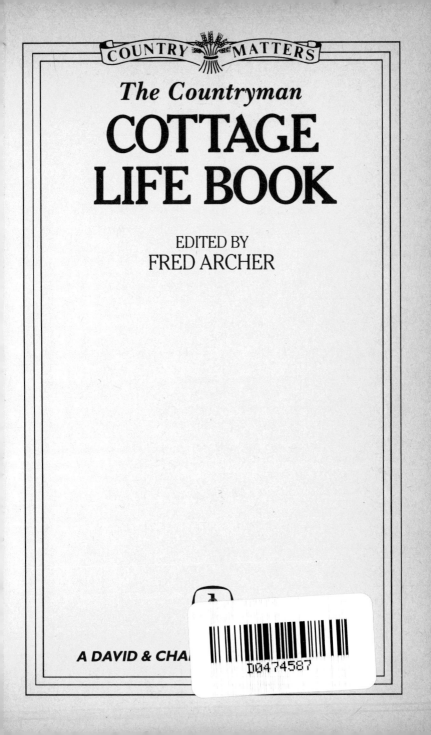

COUNTRY MATTERS

The Countryman

COTTAGE
LIFE BOOK

EDITED BY
FRED ARCHER

A DAVID & CHA

D0474587

British Library Cataloguing in Publication Data

The Countryman cottage life book.
   1. Great Britain. Rural regions. Social life.
   I. Archer, Fred, 1915-
   941.009'734

   ISBN 0-7153-9250-6

First published in 1974 in hardback by David & Charles
(Holdings) Limited. This paperback edition published 1988
by David & Charles Publishers plc
and printed in Great Britain by
Redwood Burn Limited, Trowbridge, Wiltshire
for David & Charles Publishers plc
Brunel House   Newton Abbot   Devon

Cover photographs
Front: Cottage and garden in Little Miserden, Buckinghamshire.
          Edifice/Darley.
Back: Thatcher at work in North Poorton, Dorset *'Britain on
          View' (BTA/ETB).*

Contents

CONTENTS

1 Cottage Characters

My Poacher **by H. E. Bates**

A letter from a friend tells me that Buck is dead and that there is something in the papers about him. But the fact that he had done time and had been a great poacher is not published. He was famous, as fame went in those days, before I was born. Though I must have seen him hundreds of times, I spoke to him once only. He was a very big man, fifteen or sixteen stone. In his prime, which must have been in the nineties, he probably never weighed more than thirteen, perhaps even less. He could hardly have afforded to weigh more. For though he was a shoemaker by profession, and a fine shoemaker too, and a prizefighter by necessity, he was a poacher by instinct. And that meant he was also an athlete. The poacher of today travels by car, even by bus or lorry. Buck travelled on foot. His poaching grounds, the parks of neighbouring castles and mansions, were fifteen miles off. Today that means nothing. To Buck it meant a night walk of over thirty miles, with the gutted and often ungutted rabbits weighing him down on the homeward journey, the furlongs changing into miles and the miles to leagues as the rabbits grew heavier and heavier. And that on a good night, with luck. On a bad night, with the keepers out, it meant that the homeward journey became not a walk, but a run, the rabbits dumped perhaps to make the going lighter. And since keepers can also run it would very often mean a fight in the darkness. So that Buck can hardly have carried any excessive weight in his prime. Even in his later years he was very solid. There was no appearance of looseness, no belly, no seediness. The hardness of the poaching, prize-fighting days never left him. He walked very upright, rather slowly, with the

5

typical ponderous muscular swagger of his age and his class, his hands thrust into his trouser-belt, his shoemaker's bowler tilted back, his legs apart, the smoky clay stuck close under the end of his nose. He could spit on a flea: the long swift nonchalant spit of a careless artist.

Going to school one morning, with a pair of very new brown shoes on, I met Buck. Brown shoes, not boots, were then only just coming into vogue, and there was something still a little effeminate about them. I was very proud of mine. Buck said good morning to me. He said good morning to everyone. 'Good morning,' I said. He took one long sardonic look at me. And then he said, 'Brown shoes.' No more. But it was a masterly stroke of contempt which I shall never forget. Not that Buck was ever, I think, vindictive. He was famous for the richness and spontaneity of his humour. Wherever Buck appeared there was laughter. He was comic. He bawled affectionate and tenderly droll remarks to strange young women across the street. His voice was immense, truly Falstaffian, so that his private remarks were public and his public utterances universal. And it was his voice and his humour that gave him, more than all his poaching and fighting, the glory that he enjoyed. The respectable and often bloodless life of the new Midland towns threw Buck into comic and robust relief. And he accepted the new life. He was a great picture-goer, and his bawled asides, in the sudden hushes preceding the close-ups of cinema love, were famous. And finally, as is so often the case with extremely physical types, he was most tender with children. The character of his humour, often gross, only changed in order to become fantastic. And so I heard a little girl say to him, as all little girls said to him: 'What'd you have today for dinner, Mr Buck?' And heard him reply, 'Plum pudden on a gold plate, my gal.'

The Stone-breaker   by B. Crocker

Half a century ago the outlook was grim for the old disabled and impecunious countryman. If totally unfit, he had nothing to look forward to but the workhouse and the pauper's uniform of drabette coat, check neckcloth and fustian trousers; but as long as he could move arms and shoulders the guardians considered him capable of breaking down block stone to road-metal size, thus saving the ratepayers at least three shillings a week. Stone breaking required skill but was nevertheless regarded as the lowest form of labour, and no able-bodied man would undertake it except of necessity. Those old-timers worked under almost impossible conditions. On Sourton Down, Devon, a blind man with bruised and bleeding fingers used to break stone into the proper grades by touch. His little girl, carrying his tools, led him to his heap before she went to school and collected him at the end of the day. A man who, through neglected rheumatism, had to go to work on crutches carried his hammers in a sack slung over his shoulder. The sack acted as a cloak when it rained; there was no other shelter. A carter, both of whose legs had been broken through an accident at work, was put on to stone-breaking as soon as he could hobble with the aid of two sticks. His wife carried his tools, then went back to do the heavy work for the farmer's wife. As a road inspector I came on many such cases, so I am not one of those who sigh for the good old days.

Three Men of Wales   by R. Phillips

The three veterans whose portraits appear on page 33 were all in their late eighties. Thomas Jones, bottom left, eldest of eleven children, was born in a mud-walled house on the slopes of Llanddewi Brefi in Cardiganshire. Apart from one brief interlude in the South Wales coalfield, he worked hard on the land all his life. In religion, education and rural development he was a reformer. Fifty years ago he was one of an enthusiastic and gallant band of pioneers who inculcated the principles of agricultural co-operation in the hearts of their fellow countrymen. At eighty-five years of age, with his own hands, he sank a 20-ft well by his cottage door in order to ensure a supply of water for his successors. His faith in the future may not then have been as strong as his

7

love for the past, but as he approached his ninetieth birthday he barely conceded 'Thy Kingdom come', for he knew that Thomas Jones had to help to make that possible.

John Davies, at the top, was also born and bred in the poor hill-country of West Wales where he returned to end his days. He was a tailor by trade and clothed his contemporaries, first on farms and later in the mining valleys. His income, though small, was always fairly safe, for the people had to be clothed and to wear something special at weddings and funerals. When eventually his eyesight failed him, his face remained free of lines and nothing could alter its serenity as the years passed.

Lewis Morgan, on the right, was short and stocky. When work was scarce on farms and in the mines, there was always a job for a strong healthy vigorous man who could shift things, and as a navvy Lewis Morgan could lift weights that other men could hardly move. After strong beer in rough company he stood up to bruisers and bullies; his reach was short and footwork clumsy, but he had a powerful punch. When he was nearly ninety years of age his mind and memory retained all their activity, but he needed a stick to steady himself as he moved slowly from the hearth to the sunshine outside his doorway. Rheumatism had destroyed the power of his muscular thighs and taken the strength from his sturdy legs. As his heart was sound, so his nature was kind. When economic forces drove him from home, he went, but in the end he returned to live among his own people.

Workhouse Child   by Lily Maher

I was born in Tanner Street, Northampton, in the year 1877. My father worked on the railway until he was knocked down and killed by a train in Hunsbury Hill Tunnel. On his death, my mother, a native of Daventry, married the lodger and this caused my eldest brother to leave home as he was of the same age as our step-father. I was the youngest of four children; the other three were boys.

We now returned to Daventry and my mother earned money

by sewing toe-caps on the tops of shoes from Stead and Simpson's factory; she fixed the tops in what they called a 'clam' and sewed them with wax-end. I think I was between three and four years old at the time she died of TB. I remember than an aunt came from Bedford to my mother's funeral, and that my step-father persuaded her to take me back to live with her. We went by horse-drawn coach from Daventry to Weedon as the railway was not yet made. Anyway, my aunt got tired of me and I had to go back to my step-father. He then sent me to a cousin at Northampton, but she soon tired of me, and back I had to go. There was a man who used to visit the public house in our street. He had two daughters living with him and he took me home, but one of the daughters brought me back the same night, and gave me a little threepenny piece.

After that I was on my own. Father would leave me some food on the table every morning before he went to work; I used to run round to a neighbour's house with my clothes, to be dressed. Then, one day he asked a Mrs T if she would look after me, promising to pay her if she did and, though she kept me until she could afford to do so no longer, he never paid her one penny. Mr T also used to take work home from Stead and Simpsons, and when the time came that he had no work Mrs T said, 'Lily, I am afraid I shall have to put you in the workhouse, as Mr T has no work to do.' So she took me there, and from that day on my life was changed.

I had been in the workhouse for some time when one day I was fetched into a room where the Board of Guardians were sitting. They called a lady into the room. She wanted a little girl and they asked her if she would have me. She said she could not have me because her husband would not like the colour of my hair, which was auburn. Another lady was then called into the room and they asked her the same question. She said, 'The child can't help the colour of her hair.' And with that I was boarded out at Badby.

The lady, Mrs B, lived at the Woodyard on the Church Green.

9

She was paid 3s 6d per week for my food, and 10s every three months for my clothes. I went to Badby School and the workhouse paid for my schooling: 2d a week. Mrs B brought me up to work: I used to clean floors, fetch the water from a brook for drinking and cleaning; I used to go 'sticking' and picking up leaves to use as litter for the pigs in winter. Sometimes I used to get up early to go to Fawsley to buy venison dripping, six-pennyworth at a time.

In the summer I went out to gather dandelions, coltsfoot, cowslips and primroses, all to make wine. In the autumn after I came home from school and during the holidays I used to go picking up acorns and people would come to buy them for their pigs, but Mrs B never gave me any of the money.

In the evenings, I knitted black stockings for myself and Mrs B, and for Mr B, blue ones with white tops, so I was always at work. The only time that Mrs B gave me money was at Daventry 'Mop', when she gave me twopence and let me go to spend it.

During the August holidays I would go gleaning with Mrs B and we would get a lot of corn which was ground for the pigs and so on. Sometimes she would bake her own bread, and then I would ask her to bake me a lardy cake, which I liked very much. The baking was done in a 'stick' oven outside the house. In readiness for the baking I used to take a little milk-can and twopence to a lady's house on my way to school, for the balm which the carrier left, and I would call for this on my way home at teatime.

I went to school until I was about ten or eleven years of age and when the time came for me to leave the relieving officer came to see Mrs B. He told her that his wife kept a registry office and would like me to go and work for her, so that she could see what sort of a situation would be best for me. They had a family of children and I was there for about eighteen months. I was very happy there. The only thing that troubled me was that he came home drunk most Fridays, and would knock his wife about and turn me out of the house. This was after he had been round the villages taking money to the old people. His sister-in-law lived next door, and I would stay there that night and go back the next morning.

One evening he came back from his village round and gave me a month's notice, and told me to go home. After that they had a girl straight from the workhouse. He started to turn her out on Friday nights, but she did not go next door as I had done, and back next morning. No, she went straight back to the workhouse and reported him, so he got the sack. The last I heard of them was that they had gone abroad.

Of course, I went back to Badby, to Mrs B. The neighbour told Mrs B that she had a daughter living in a village near Market Drayton, in Shropshire, and she was sure that I should have a good home with her. They were bakers. Mrs B took me in the carrier's cart to Daventry Station—and I was to be sure to ask for Newport, Salop—and the family met me with a pony and trap, as it was a long way to the little village, called Cheswardine.

I had a terrible life with them. I had to get up early, as I had to clean two rooms before they got up: sweep, dust, black-lead the grates, light the fires and get the breakfast. I remember one morning I was crying because I could not get the fire to burn. The man next door heard me and asked what was the matter, and then came in to help.

I think people were sorry for me. I used to have to fetch water from a deep well that had a bucket and chain, across the road from where I lived. Sometimes it was late when I had to go, and an old lady that lived near the well would put a lighted candle in her window so that I could see, and she would come out and help me. She used to say that they had no business to send me: 'the Master should get the water'. Sometimes in the winter there was ice round the well, which she said was very deep, but she could not say anything to them as she was living in one of their old thatched cottages.

The Mistress made cakes to sell in the shop, and her husband took some to sell on the rounds with the bread. I had to help with making the bread, as well as doing the housework. The bakehouse was away from the house and at night she would go to bed, but I had to go with him to the bakehouse to put the yeast and salt in a bucket of warm water while he mixed it into the flour. The only time I sat down in the house was when I had my meals. She always found me something to do in the evenings, as they had three children. There were shoes to clean and knives and forks and other items. At last I decided that I could not put up with the treatment any longer. The Mistress had been hitting me because I did not say 'please' to the Master when I asked him to help me shake the carpets. I said to her, 'You are always saying you are going to send me home. Now I will go home,' and I went upstairs to pack my tin box.

She followed me up and told me that I must give her one month's notice. I knew that was right, and I also knew that I should have to get someone to take me to the station if I was going to leave. Soon after this she told me that she had received a letter from Mrs B, saying that she would not have me back home. This hurt me very much.

I was very worried to hear that Mrs B would not have me back, so I decided to write to her and ask her what I was to do. I wrote and posted it without anyone knowing, and Mrs B wrote straight back, telling me I was to come home and to be sure I brought all my clothes. The Cheswardine people never said anything when they knew I had heard from Badby and the day came when they took me in the pony and trap to Newport Station, and so I returned 'home'.

I stayed at home for a week; then I heard of a lady in Byfield wanting a maid. Mrs S asked me if I could cook: I said, 'No, but I am willing to learn,' so she engaged me on the condition that my character was all right. I came to Byfield 8 May 1893. I stayed with Mrs S for two years and learnt to cook her way. They kept a draper's shop and the time came when she would come into the kitchen to tell me what they wanted for dinner, and leave me to do it while she helped in the shop.

I spent a very happy two years there, and I was sorry to leave, but on 22 September 1895, I got married. I wasn't much over eighteen when I married and I had only £7 in the bank. My husband had no money. When my first baby arrived I was very ill; my cousin in Northampton bought a bundle of baby clothes for me from a pawnbroker's shop. I still had the christening gown in the year 1968.

For a time things were very bad for us. My husband could only get work a day at a time—when the farmer was threshing corn for instance. He was a good worker when he could get it. I had a baby every two years until 1921, and I brought eleven children up, all born in Byfield. The year we moved from our little wedding cottage to another one with a garden and a pigsty was a turning-point for us: the railway was being made at Woodford Halse, and my husband, Jack, got a job on the railway. We never looked back again. We took some allotment land and grew wheat, and from it I used to make my own bread, taking the dough down to the bakehouse before my children were up.

One day my eldest little boy came home and said to me, 'The boys asked me, "Why don't your mother sell us some sweets?" ' We had just sold a little pig to the butcher and I had half a sovereign left upstairs, so I went to Northampton and bought some sweets: they had to be ones that I could count, as I had no scales. I got a box of Woodbine cigarettes: they were a penny for a packet of five. Sweets were 2oz for 1d, and tobacco 3d for 1oz. I started my shop on 5 July 1907—the birthday of one of my babies.

My husband worked on the railway, right up to his death in 1923. He never went to a pub, and was very careful with his money. What money we saved we put into the Post Office. He died from Bright's Disease. He left me with five little children, four of them going to school, and the baby not able to walk. While my husband was at home ill I found my shop a very great help. Afterwards, I got 10s a week from the Government and 3s a week from a Railway Orphan Fund.

I stayed in business until 1941. Afterwards I missed the shop very much, and I missed my young son, too, when he got married and left me alone. I then took in a gentleman boarder who was a bachelor. He had come to be a porter at Byfield railway station and his name was Michael Maher. After a time he asked me to marry him; he was wanting a home and someone to look after him, so I changed my name from Mrs John Smith to Mrs Michael Maher and we lived very happily together for twelve years. We were married in September 1944, and he died in October 1956. I have eight children left out of my family of eleven—all married—and they are scattered all over the country, one in Northern Ireland. All have got families. I have five grand-daughters married.

On my ninetieth birthday my friends in the village made it a very happy day for me, with fruit and flowers. It really was very nice, but I was disappointed because I had to have tea on my own. Not one of my family could be with me, and I have not got over my disappointment yet. Now I live in the Danetre Hospital, Daventry, and I have just passed my ninety-fourth birthday.

Mrs Maher was looking forward eagerly to seeing her life-story 'printed in a book' in The Countryman. *She was as lively as usual until she suddenly became ill and her children were called to her bedside. She died on 4 February 1972. The funeral service, held in the Congregational Chapel, Byfield, was attended by over thirty of her children and grandchildren, and she was buried in the village churchyard under a drift of the spring flowers that she had always loved.*

A Bit o' Fire   by Dominic Reeve

Some little time ago I went to visit an old travelling woman who had just moved into a council house on the edge of a large town in the south of England. She had been living in an old waggon on a local common and the council had forced her to leave it, although neither she nor her family had any desire to move from accommodation which they had found quite adequate and comfortable.

On arriving at her new abode I banged vigorously on the composition board of both front and back doors without result; and I was about to leave when I saw the figure of old Mary Jaynette crouched over a small fire at the bottom of her garden. She appeared to be frying bacon, and her black kettle was hanging from its crane; her teapot and a small traveller-style food cupboard were beside her. There she sat cross-legged on the ground, smoking her pipe and watching the bacon frying. She smiled as I approached. 'Ar, my son,' she said, 'I shall never make me mind happy bidin' all day in that dear house. I'd sooner have me ole-fashioned ways an' me bit o' fire outside on the ground. You cain't beat a bit o' fire, can you, my son?'

They Dined Out by W. R.

Jake served my father faithfully as gamekeeper in the North Riding of Yorkshire, rarely taking a day off and never venturing farther than the near-by market town. At the end of his fiftieth year of service my father suggested some celebration and was surprised when the old man said he would like a trip to London. 'Ye see, sir,' he explained, 'I've allus wanted ter see one o' them Lunnon restrunts, an' I wouldn't arf tell 'em about it at t' local.'

So London it was, and when the great day arrived my mother took me down to the station to see them off. Jake was dressed for the occasion, his Homburg at a jaunty angle, his old-fashioned frock-coat green with age but brightened by a mauve celluloid dicky and a red spotted tie. Under his arm he carried a large gig umbrella, and in his hand he clutched a straw basket, or 'bass' as it was called in Yorkshire, the lid tied down with string. On arriving in London my father suggested that Jake might like to leave his luggage at the hotel before doing a little sightseeing, but he would have none of it; where he went the basket went too, though he was at length persuaded to leave the umbrella under the bed for safety.

All eyes seemed to be on the pair as they entered a well-known restaurant and made their way to a table at the far end of the room, but the gamekeeper was quite unaware of the interest he was causing. Seating himself at the table with his basket on his knee, he tied a napkin round his neck, with his beard carefully arranged outside. 'Hi, young man,' he called to a waiter, 'fetch us a couple o' plates an' be sharp about it. Git on with it an' don't look so gormless, lad.'

The surprised waiter soon returned with two plates, and Jake's great moment had arrived. Dumping the basket on the table, he opened it with a flourish, took out two beautifully cooked partridges and, to my father's horror, placed them with all their trimmings on the plates. 'I never did trust them foreigners,' he said, gazing proudly at the birds, 'so I says to the wife Polly, cook us summat dacent ter eat; me an' Boss don't want ter starve while we're in Lunnon.' And he tackled the meal with relish, grabbing the bird between his fingers and tearing the flesh from the bones with his teeth. Nothing must be wasted, for it would be an insult to Polly to leave a morsel.

By the time the staff had recovered themselves and decided on a cover charge, my father had grabbed Jake's arm and dragged him from the place, not slackening speed until they were lost in the London crowd.

If the adventure had not turned out quite as he had expected, at least Jake was satisfied, and for both it would be a day to remember.

John, a Peasant   by Richard North

John was born at Stoke Mandeville, near Aylesbury, within sight of the highest point of the Chilterns, and he died at the age of seventy-nine in 1915. He lived all his life in the same small mean house that he and his father had rented for more than a century. It was for a long time infested with black beetles, and contained many things common enough in John's day—a candle box, a lantern glazed with horn, pattens, and apparatus for straw plaiting. It was never lit by anything but candles. Two pairs of aged eyes and ten pairs of young ones endured the strain of reading or working by a single light. 'Two candles a-burnin' an' never a plough a-gooin' ' was a frequent expression if a second candle was carried from another room and inadvertently left alight. Outside were an open hovel for the cart, a stable for the pony, and a 'woodus' (wood-house) which contained the odoriferous gleanings of John's business. Like his father, he was a marine store dealer, a hawker and a carrier. Beyond the vegetable garden was a small paddock where his pony grazed. A tiny flower garden by the wall of the house provided his wife with one of her few pleasures. John lived in the days of turnpikes, and paid tolls. Somewhere among his small wardrobe there was a smock-frock. He had seen a public execution.

John was short and wiry, and he looked straight and continuously into the eyes of those with whom he spoke. His lips were thin and suggested cruelty; his ears were lobeless and exceedingly small; his nose was straight and pointed; and his rich brown eyes turned a cold look on the world. His beard hung all over his face and throat. In the most casual contacts John's character revealed downrightness, certainty, rigidity, and he would talk across a social gap with an independence of utterance and a readiness to contradict that were in contrast with the timidity of his fellow villagers. But he would not allow himself to be called 'Mr'. 'Plain John is me name; you call me John.' The vicar's wife had a tongue of repute, and was no mean foe. Once when he considered that she had made a reflection on his character he said: 'She shan't say that; I'll goo an' see 'er; gimme my best jackut'—and off he went and subdued the vicarage. His modest estimate of his essential needs was a knife, a bit of string and a shilling, which three things he held a man ought always to have about him.

John's boots were made so that they could be worn on either foot. He wore them on different feet on alternate days. These boots, liberally greased in wet weather, were so big that he could wear not only a pair of stockings but a pair or two of stocking feet. He walked with his feet pointing so much outwards that the yokels called him 'the dew-spreader'.

John wore double-breasted waistcoats, being apprehensive of catching cold, and would never step outside the door without a hat, or have his hair cut in the winter. He had a theory that he could keep well only by the constant use of Epsom salts. Saltpetre he believed to be excellent for the kidneys, and cold tea for tired eyes. He would bathe the closed lids at night, grope his way to bed, and go to sleep without opening them again.

He married a girl who in her youth had fine proportions, a queenly carriage, and good looks, and the pair had eleven children who became so scattered over the globe that they never all met together.

The loss of respectability through debt was the dread of John and his wife. They would never buy what they could not pay for. There was, however, one occurrence which seared John's conscience. After an illness that reduced him to his very last coin, he began work again without renewing his hawker's licence, and was caught and fined.

Until well on in life John was a heavy drinker. He would say that one wheel of the brewer's trap belonged to him. He once won a wager by drinking a bottle of brandy in an hour. He bragged that he could 'carry nine gallon o' beer—four'n a half inside an' four'n a half outside'. But eventually he was given a fright. 'I was just gettin' over the airysiplus an' the doctor looked queer at me so as I knowed there was summat in 'is mind, an' I ses "Out wi' it, doctor, if ye got anything to say. What is it? Be I a-drinkin' too much?" "John," 'e ses, "if you goo on like this for another twel' month you'll be dead or in a lunatic asylum." "Doctor," I ses, "I'll never touch another drop as long as I live!" An' I've kep' me word.'

When he used to come home intoxicated he would think nothing of turning the children out of doors; and his wife often delivered the goods and unharnessed and fed the pony when he was incapable of doing it. Not until she was advanced in life was she able to indulge in a recreation of which she was fond—reading. I have seen her with *Paradise Lost*. A circumstance that surprised not only her family but also the village was that she continued to drink beer after he had given it up. Every night of her life the 'Bull' supplied her with half a pint, which she warmed in a saucepan and drank with her bread and cheese.

I ought to have mentioned that though he might be drunk six days of the week, John would never touch a drop on Sundays. Although he drank, he never swore and he never smoked. 'There, put that pipe out; I wun't 'ave no smokin' 'ere,' was a command to some members of his family. Sunday trading he also thought sinful. He has refused, with abuse, to sell a candle on a Sunday to an old woman who had forgotten to replenish her stock on Saturday. 'Sarve ye right,' he said. 'I wun't let ye 'ave it of a Sunday. If ye can't think o' yer candles o' Saturday it wun't do ye no 'arm to sit in the dark or goo to bed.'

Perhaps because of the frequent 'And he rose up early in the morning' of the Old Testament, John could rise at any hour. He had, indeed, a craze for early rising. When he had to go a distance, he would start with loads of merchandise well before four o'clock, even in mid-winter.

In reference to his haberdashery hawking, a draper of Aylesbury said to John, 'Why don't you run a few more lines and start a little shop? I'd let you have the stuff on credit, and not press for the money.' 'Oh ah,' John replied; 'tha's all very well, but supposin' I di'n't sell 'em, an' at the end o' six months I 'ad your bill—where'd I be? You let me alone to goo nigglin' along in my tin-pot way, payin' twenty shillin's in the pound an' owin' nothin' to nobody.'

Upon John's gravestone is inscribed, 'His word was his bond.' A promise upon even a trivial matter was a pledge to be kept wholly and promptly. His phrase was, 'But I said I would.' A lie he regarded as the greatest of sins. 'As false as my knife' was one of his scornful epithets—the peculiar falsity of a knife being that it would as soon cut its owner as anyone else. ' 'Tis the truth as licks 'em,' he would say.

He used to tell with satisfaction the story of a policeman who was set to watch for a strawberry thief and was himself taken red-handed. But he had a sneaking regard for poachers. 'That ain't no use tryin' to stop a poacher. If 'e's after a rabbut or a pheasant 'e'll 'ave it, gamekeeper or no gamekeeper. Besides, what's a rabbut or a pheasant?'

He was impervious to argument and held with tenacity to the wildest prejudices. He once said to me, 'I wonder I ain't 'ad a smack o' th' 'ead many a time.' He was often, he said, 'as surly as a bull'. The words of a certain boaster he called 'a couple o' yards o' pump water'. John was selfish and hard on his wife. When the children who had left home returned upon visits he would say to them, 'If you be gooin' to give me anything, give it me out o' doors where yer mother can't see.' At harvest time his wife and all the children went 'leasing' in the corn fields. (The farmer would thresh a leaser's corn for the straw, and the miller would grind it for the bran.)

John brought up his children to eschew ease and to esteem diligence. ' 'E's a good feller to work' was a commendation often upon his lips. ' 'Olidays!' he would say derisively. 'I call it shameful when folks might be doin' a honest day's work.'

Not even at Christmas would John allow the children any in-dulgence that might mean a little noise; not a halfpenny could be spared for anything not eatable. The children's few pennies were pooled and spent in Aylesbury on sugar mice (at four a penny), sugar watches, and a handful of nuts. The 'tree' was a table on which these delicacies were spread out, and the children drew tickets for them out of a hat. The centre-piece and most costly article was a twopenny coconut. Such innocent enjoyment John would never allow downstairs, and the festival was celebrated in the shivering cold of the front bedroom. His method of correcting the children was to beat their backs with an ash stick. 'Come 'ere, my lord,' he would say. 'Fetch me that ash plant; take yer jackut off; take yer weskut off.' He would tell with satisfaction of his chastisement of a lad—not one of his own children—in Sunday school. 'I knocked 'im,' he'd say, 'all round that chapel, first one side an' then t'other; "I'll show ye", I ses, "who's master 'ere".'

He was content with his lot, though every day's toil was a fight to keep his independence. As he shaped with a pocket knife the wooden pegs for the cloth mops that were part of his small trading stock, he would break off from the murmuring of some hymn tune to express his gratitude for the few favours life had given him. 'Ah, my gal', he would say, 'there's many a poor creature as 'ud be glad t' 'ave what we've got. The Lord's bin good to us.'

On Sundays, if the local preacher happened to be musical, John would invite him to tea. One or two other singers were generally invited, and were hurried through their tea with reminders to look at the clock. No break in the singing was permitted till the grandfather clock or the bells of the parish church gave warning of the approach of service time. Non-participants were condemned to silence. The order was, 'Sing or be quiet; stop that clack, do!' He liked to say of his wife that he would have paid another sovereign for her if she had been musical.

There was never an hour but some melody was running through his head, and, often, finding expression on his lips. He was as enthusiastic to determine the pitch of casual sounds as Gilbert White to know whether the Selborne owls hooted in F sharp or B flat. At the chiming of a clock he would sing the note and say, 'Tha's about A, I think,' and the tuning-fork would be produced from his waistcoat pocket to test the accuracy of his ear. In childhood his voice was good, and in maturity he had a natural tenor of fine range and quality. He was wont to say that he could sing enough tenor for half a dozen basses. When over seventy he could easily and sweetly reach a top G. John could read music, and had no more difficulty with minor than with major keys. He prized this accomplishment more than his voice. A man who sang at sight, even badly, he esteemed. But I have heard him tell a man who had a fine voice and little musical sense that he was making a row 'like a bumble bee in a tar tub'. 'If you was a mile away, Bill, an' I could 'ear ye,' he said to an acquaintance, 'I could tell the first note of every bar, 'cos ye come slap on it every time an' bring it out so as everybody knows jest where ye be. An' as confident as a cock.' John's religion forbade him to countenance music that was not 'sacred'. All music not 'sacred' was 'martial', and even 'Good King Wenceslas' was prohibited. But he had difficulty in preserving the distinction where there were no words to guide him, and I have heard him commend selections from opera to which he would never have listened if he had been aware of their 'martial' character. He trained a choir at the chapel on condition that the members met for practice twice a week, wet or fine. 'I'll be there meself,' he said, ' 'ail, snow or blow'; and for eighteen years he was neither absent nor late. Once when he wanted a music book for a Sunday service, he discovered towards the end of the week that it was at a village eight miles away. That did not put him off, for on the Sunday morning he walked and fetched it. The introduction of one of 'they bellerin' organs', a harmonium, into his chapel was one of the humiliations of his life. All knowledge of the innovation was kept from him until the day before the service at which it was first played, and he shed the tears of a strong man defeated.

John once had the notion of joining the army as a cornet player. When he heard the band of the Coldstream Guards, he said, 'The man as arranges their music for 'em ought t' 'ave a pound a week as long as 'e lives. I never 'eard sich playin'. Why, once they was gooin' as fast as ever I thought they could goo, an' bless me if they di'n't all of a sudden double the pace.'

John took the greatest care of his music books and handled them caressingly. If one would not lie flat and a rough hand attempted to apply force, he would spring forward and utter a cry as if hurt. Many of these books were in manuscript, in the transcription of which he had spent laborious hours, for he was little accustomed to a pen. Their width was greater than their depth, and their cloth covers were like old leather from age and use. They were kept in a chest of drawers to which his children were forbidden access.

John was a good bell-ringer, and had rung in every belfry for miles around. He would stop and listen to a distant peal even on cold winter nights. 'That's So-and-so at number one,' he would say. 'Good ringer 'e is, never too soon an' never be'ind. But that ain't So-and-so a-ringin' number four. The chap who's got 'is bell is all over the place an' ain't got no more notion o' ringin' nor a gret gal.' Bells were church affairs, and much as he loved them they could not lure him from his Methodism; many a time he has rung in a church till within a few minutes of the service, and then dashed off to chapel.

John had a gift for games. He was fond of telling the story of his victory at a single-wicket cricket match, with one innings each and no fieldsmen. The stake was half a gallon of beer. His chief game was skittles, and in the narrow alleys so commonly found in his time on licensed premises he must have won barrel upon barrel of beer. Skittles was no child's game. The 'cheese' weighed 9lb and was tossed from a distance of 9yd. It travelled from the hand and forearm upright, or with a slight obliquity. It was projected so as to strike the first pin not centrally but a little to one side; the pin then fell to one side while the 'cheese' continued on the other, and each side of the board was cleared of further pins. If a needle were stuck into the foremost ninepin John could crush it into the wood with every throw, and he could knock down eight of the nine pins in about 90 per cent of his first throws.

' 'Ere, let me carry it,' he would say to an over-burdened woman; 'tha's too 'eavy for ye.' But I have known him cry out to a woman whose tongue had offended him, 'You want a red 'ot tater in yer mouth.' One of his sayings was, ''Tain't no use to give a apple to them as 'as got a orchard.'

John wolfed his food greedily and audibly—'golloped' it; and told with satisfied approval the story of a mother who rebuked her child, when a distinguished visitor was present, for licking its plate. 'So would you,' said the offender, 'if 'e 'adn't bin 'ere.' At breakfast he would eat quantities of cold fat meat or cold meat pudding or pie. He had only one other meal in the day, for his motto was not 'little and often' but 'much and seldom'. On Sundays he would have a tea meal, and he would never in any circumstances be satisfied with two cups or indulge himself with four. He liked his meat underdone. 'Jest pop it in the pan, turn it over, an' fetch it out; I can't abear t' 'ave all the goodness cooked out o' me meat.' Veal he despised. 'I can't see nothin' at all in that; let it grow till it gets to beef is what I say.' His utilitarianism made him despise table-cloths; they cost money and made work, and 'ye can't ate 'em.' He would often turn back his corner of the cloth and put his plate on the bare table to the annoyance of his wife, who would say, 'Ye might jest as well ate yer grub out of a pig tro'.'

He never gave his wife the least assistance in the home. He was careless and untidy, and expected to be waited upon. He could not even brush his hair without asking, ' 'Ave I got that partin' straight?' He was conscious of these failings, and said that he wished to die before his wife. 'She could git along better wi'out me nor I could wi'out 'er.'

He would never allow that the weather was hot; 'warm' or 'very warm' was the most he would say—though on the hottest days he would be seen with a cabbage leaf protuding from the back of his hat and hanging down his neck. Bad weather he thought of in regard to its effect upon his poor neighbours. 'This weather 'as kep' poor So-and-so out o' work for a week; dunno what 'e'll do, poor feller, wi' 'is family. Snow may look perty, but you jest think 'ow many folks it'll put out o' work.'

A good piece of hedging would always attract his attention. 'Now, jest you look at that,' he would say. 'I can tell who done that, though I never see 'im at it. Tha's Barnet Spittles's work. There ain't a man anywhere near 'ere as can touch 'im.' Similarly he would praise George Bates's ricks. 'Bootiful, I call 'em. You can walk all round 'em, an' ye can't see no difference wherever ye stand.' On another man's work his remark was, 'Some gret slummackin' gal might 'a' bilt it.' Of Jimmy Dorrell's management of a scythe he said, ' 'E's sich a good whet, ye see. A man could perty near shave 'isself wi' Jimmy's scythe. There's plenty o' men as can mow but can't whet. There's more in whettin' nor in mowin'.'

He detested dogs, and was in the habit of carrying a rabbit's foot or two in his pocket wherewith to propitiate the fiercest of them. 'There never wus a dog yit as 'ud bite ye if ye listened to its master,' was his view. 'If I 'ad my way there'd be no more dogs than there is queens.' He also hated bees.

At sixty-five John broke down. With his club superannuation, the earnings of his wife, and some help from the children, his house was free from actual distress. Later there were the old-age pensions. From the time of his retirement from work his strength of character steadily declined. He died of a paralytic stroke.

South-Country Customs   by L. N. Graburn

I used to know a wheelwright and undertaker who died in a Sussex village just before World War I at well over eighty years of age. He was the great bee-man of the district, and all round his garden there were straw skeps on stools made from the rough elm slabs from which coffin boards had been cut; the legs were old waggon-wheel spokes painted red. When he put a swarm in a skep, he plastered it round with cow-dung to keep out the draught. (In the West Country stone slabs were used instead of elm wood.) He used also to follow the old custom of giving a stock or swarm of bees to a newly married couple—a common present in the days before sugar, when honey was the only sweetener.

As a small boy, he had been allowed to accompany his father, who had also been an undertaker, when he and his man were carrying a coffin to the cottage of a shepherd. The widow and her daughter were much distressed, because the shepherd had been to church on only very rare occasions since his wedding day sixty years earlier; so the undertaker's man said, 'I reckon 'e ought to be buried with a piece of wool in 'is 'and—same as all shepherds was years ago.' While the coffin was being taken upstairs, the boy was sent to the chalky road leading to the downs to collect some of the wool which was there in plenty on the brambles. On his return he saw his father put the wool in the shepherd's hand, which pleased the widow immensely. This ancient custom was, of course, to show the man's calling and to excuse him to his Maker for absences from Divine Service. It is still carried on in some eastern countries, but this was probably one of the last occasions, little more than a century ago, when the rite was performed here in Britain.

The Compleat Bachelor   by the Roadman

One day I were breakin' stones. There was a purty smart wind a-blowin' and the leaves was fallin' all caterwise and skitterwaisen when I seed Mrs Penny come pankin' along head to wind. She pulled up an' says: 'Ah! Jarge, there you be! Why I been a-thinkin' and a-thinkin' of ye, and turning ye over in my mind-like. Why ain't ye never got married? Did you never ask naun?' 'No,' I says, 'I never did, but they've asked me dunnamany times. There was one old gal when I wore a young chap she said she'd be pleased to do for me. Says she "You, wants someone to cook for ye and darn your stockings—and think o' the dust as u'll gather in your dwellin' with no woman there to clean up for ye!" I answers: 'I likes the dust to lay, 'tis healthier than flirtin all about and gettin' in your neck. If I has holes in my stockings my boots hides 'em, so 'tis a grievous waste of time to goo darnin'. As for cookin' I be a better cook nor any woman. I can make fleed cakes 'nuff to knock their heads off, and I don't want you doin' any chores inside my doors; don't you dare try meddlin' wi' me!' So she never did again. Then there was a party justabout vinegar behind her smilin' teeth, she kep' hintin' to me what a mort o' money she had to her name in the bank, till at last I says, 'I be a man as likes to be lonesome; I be a still man; I won't be chid nor bid by any. Peace is what I wants and will have. What does the Book say? " 'Tis better to have a dinner o' yarbs with peace, than a dish o' tongues all spikes an' no peace." If your temper be half as sharp's your nose I pity them as has to do with ye.' So she gave me no more sheep's eye. Folks must allus be interferin'. Why old parson he stops one day and he says: 'Jarge, my good man, you'd be better off married, more comformable-like, why don't ye?' I answers, 'I couldn't abide to 'live long o' a grey mare same as you, sir, and thankee much.' He coughs very loud, marching off with he's cheeks a-lookin' like the purple apoplexy. Then Mrs Penny she stutters, 'I allow that wore impersome of ye.' And I says, 'All the same, Mrs Penny, though I thanks ye for your interest, may I make so bold as to ask ye if you be a-perposing to me in your own lil way?' 'You owdacious old image you!' she skreels. 'Just because I wore neighbourly in thinkin' o' ye you've the high vanity to fancy I'd marry such an old ammut, and have a slommacky bacca-smellin' old tom-turkey like you scambling and spannelling about my dentical lil cottage? You sassy old rabbit.' Yaas, Mrs Penny she got middlin' rough and reglar rudy, but I took to hittin' up the largest stones so's I couldn't hear what she wore sayin', an' by'n by she flows down the road looking unaccountable uppish an' blumble-some. Aah!

2 Cottage Crafts and Industry

Dorset Buttons   **by Marian E. Chappell**

In the eighteenth century the cottage industry of 'buttony' was widespread in north-east and east Dorset. About 1690 Abraham Case, a native of Shaftesbury, invented a new type of button, possibly to circumvent a law of 1685. In order to protect the metal-button trade in Birmingham, this forbade the making of cloth-covered buttons; and it remained on the statute book until 1727. The new type of button, known as 'cloth-work', could scarcely have been called 'cloth-covered' because, although it had a linen centre, it was covered with fine lace-stitchery. Refugee Huguenot lace-workers in the north-east of the county took to the work, and their fine lace-thread was used in many of the early buttons.

The first cloth-work button, based on a ring of Dorset sheep-horn, was known as a 'high top'. A piece of linen cloth was pulled in a twist, so that it formed a firm conical shape with the horn as its base. Over the linen was worked a kind of chain stitch which went round and round, the loops being so arranged that they came underneath each other down the sides of the button from tip to base. The secret of making this button has been lost, and indeed how the smallest were contrived at all is a puzzle. They ranged from about half an inch high and a quarter of an inch across the base down to something like one-fifth of an inch high and three-twentieths across. The high top was popular for gentlemen's hunting waistcoats and would last a lifetime.

Next, about 1715, came the 'Dorset knob', a development of the high top; although much flatter and broader, it was made in much the same way. The buttonhole ring or 'bird's-eye' followed. This was quite stiff and firm but, when taken apart, has been found to be based only on a piece of cloth cut on the bias, firmly twisted, formed into a ring and tightly buttonholed over. It may perhaps be regarded as a transitional type of button, the ring of horn having disappeared.

Peter Case, a grandson of Abraham, invented a quite different type of button about 1750; it was based on a wire ring made of a special alloy which did not rust. First came the 'singleton', slightly padded in the centre and covered with linen cloth. Some were back-stitched round on the inner side of the ring, some had

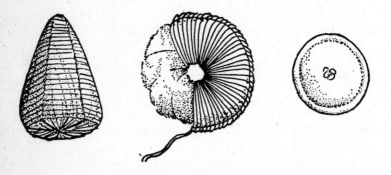

High top (c 1700), bird's-eye partly undone to show construction and mid-eighteenth-century singleton, all about over natural size

two rows of back-stitching and others, more rarely, were button-holed round over the ring. In the middle were different patterns composed of groups of french knots, which might be from three to seven in number.

The singleton, probably used largely for shirts, led directly to the button which became so widely known for a century and is still recognised as the typical Dorset button. It is based on a wire ring and has a worked centre. The wire ring was made in many cottage homes in the north and east of the county, and even over the border in Somerset and Wiltshire, during the second half of the eighteenth century and the first half of the nineteenth. The wire was brought from Birmingham in great waggons with broad-rimmed wheels which could carry loads of a ton to 30cwt. It was cut into various lengths and then made into rings by specially trained boys and girls known as 'winders and dippers'. They twisted the wire round a spindle, then soldered the ends together. The rings were tied into gross lots by 'stringers'.

The ring was first covered with buttonhole stitch, and this was called 'casting'. The knots on the outside were then smoothed inwards by children with a wood or bone 'slicker'. Thread was wound across the diagonal of the ring again and again, care being taken to cross exactly in the middle. This was known as 'laying'. Then the crossed threads were caught with two stitches in the middle, one up and down, one across, to fix them. Finally, the centre was filled in with one of several designs, which gave the buttons their names. Some were called 'Dorset crosswheel', 'old Dorset', 'Blandford cartwheel', 'honeycomb' and 'basketweave'. There was a name for each size too. The tiniest, a bare three-sixteenths of an inch across, was a 'mite'; some of the larger ones were 'waistcoats' and 'outsizes'. Buttons which had become dirty in the working were boiled in a linen bag. The finished products were mounted in gross lots on cards covered with paper of different colours according to quality. Yellow was for the cheapest, dark blue for a better quality and pink for export only. Very few of the pink remain today.

Between 1830 and 1850 the button makers were paid 1s 8d to 3s 6d a gross according to quality, the finished products being taken by women to certain picking-up spots or to agents. In 1952 an old lady, then ninety-two, told how women used to walk the ten miles from Margaret Marsh to Blandford with buttons; half-way there was a house where they called for a rest and bread and cheese and beer usually paid for by the agent.

There were agents at Shaftesbury, Blandford, Sherborne, Bere Regis, Poole, Langton Matravers, Tarrant Keyneston and elsewhere. At the Milborne Stileham agency, set up by Peter Case Jr in 1803, buttons were accepted each Friday, when the place is said to have been crowded 'like a fair'. In the more remote districts agents called at fixed times at collecting points. Payment was not always made in money, but sometimes in goods.

Towards the end of the eighteenth century Lady Caroline Damer of Milton Abbey established a school for twelve poor children, who were clothed and taught reading spinning and buttony. In 1812 a Mr Acheson is said to have been the chief employer of labour, to the extent of 1,200 women and children. During the first three or four weeks children received no pay, for they 'spoiled much thread'. They then received a penny a day for two months, and a shilling a week for two more months. Eventually the best hands could earn as much as 10s to 12s a week. Buttony was unpopular with farmers because it was difficult to get women and children to work for ninepence a day in the fields.

In the 1840s a London office in Addle Street had an annual turnover of £10,000 to £12,000. In addition to sales in England, Scotland and Wales, buttons were exported to all the principal cities of Europe and to Boston, Quebec and New York. A member

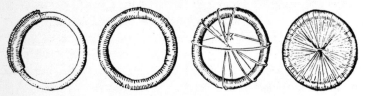

Four stages of Dorset cartwheel

of the Case family who had gone to Liverpool to oversee the export trade made a fortune, which enabled him to build Case Street and Clayton Square in that city. Mrs Jackson of Shaftesbury, who has done so much in the past fifteen years to revive the craft, received from America a sketch of a card which appeared to show the coasts of England and America with ships on the ocean between them. To different parts of the card, on the ships, sails and so on, various samples of Dorset buttons were fastened. She believes that an agent sent this out as a sample card.

With the invention, by one Ashton, of a button-making machine, which was shown at the Great Exhibition of 1851, trade fell away dramatically. The last large order fulfilled by a Case is said to have been one valued at £850 in 1859. By the end of the century the cottage industry had almost completely disappeared. All memories of it, too, might have vanished, if Florence, Dowager Lady Lees had not then sought to revive the craft at Lytchett Minster. While people who had been actively engaged in buttony were still alive, she scoured the county for information and had all the traditional wire-ring designs copied. Variations were also added. The 'spangle' was a cartwheel with tiny sequins round the rim; the 'gem' resembled a wooden bead wrapped round with silk thread, then embroidered longitudinally. The 'yarrell', a development of the crosswheel and some inch and a quarter across, was used as an election button in red or blue. The bird's-eye of Edwardian times was formed on a shaped circle of wood with a hole at the centre, instead of a ring of twisted cloth. Many of these Edwardian buttons were made with silk thread, and orders were often given to match materials for evening dresses. The trade in them was good until World War I. I have a vague recollection of seeing cards of buttons for sale in a tiny cottage window at Lytchett about 1910.

In 1931 Mrs Jackson and her husband bought for conversion two cottages in the hamlet of Twyford, near Shaftesbury. This small place has, as she puts it, neither church nor shop, post office nor public house; yet her two cottages were numbered 54 and 55. This high numbering made her curious, and inquiries among the inhabitants disclosed that, a century earlier, this had been a large and thriving village devoted to buttony. The collapse of the craft had brought poverty and starvation to Twyford, where whole families had been engaged in it. So acute did the problem become that the Government transferred many of them—350 people from the Shaftesbury area alone—to Australia,

Canada, Tasmania and other oversea territories. It would be interesting to know of any traditional stories told by descendants of these families. Their deserted English homes eventually crumbled away; but in various places, before war-time ploughing, garden trees and shrubs marked the sites.

Ever since, Mrs Jackson has been acquiring information on Dorset buttons. Four years ago interest in the subject was given a further impetus when an elderly lady who was giving up her home handed over a trunk full of the buttons, antique and modern, to Madeline Lady Lees, the late dowager. She had had this collection ever since the earlier Lady Lees had bought up the remaining stock when the last agency came to an end in 1908 on the death of old William Case, the last surviving member of the family that had invented and promoted the Dorset button.

Now it is possible to buy both antique and Edwardian buttons; and not only these. Mrs Jackson and her pupils make modern buttons to match a wardrobe; and you can learn to make them for yourself.

The Horse Doctor   by John T. Cantlay

Minty died recently in his ninetieth year, and the parishes of Cruden and Slains in Aberdeenshire will miss his raw-boned gangling figure, always with a big black collie close at heel. He was by trade a slaughterman, which gave him his first insight into the anatomy of farm animals. He also acquired a long scar from elbow to wrist—the result of his contracting the dread disease of anthrax. The doctor saw little hope of recovery but did his best by cutting out the affected part and cauterising the wound with a red-hot iron. It was all done without anaesthetic, the patient being firmly tied down and given a bottle of whisky to suck.

When Minty married he rented a small farm and found that he had a gift for helping calving cows and lambing sheep. Neighbours were soon calling on him to assist with difficult cases. My earliest recollection of Minty is of seeing him stripped to the skin, sprawled in the 'greep' behind a cow, getting the calf into the proper position for delivery. He was very gentle, as many big men are, and his great strength permitted him to continue long after a lesser man would have had to give up.

He taught me how to 'drog' or give a bottle of medicine to any farm animal; and I was very proud when, under his tuition, I managed to administer a 'ball' to a horse. I had to insert my left hand into its mouth and pull the tongue well out. Then, holding the ball between the first and third fingers, with the second finger on top and the thumb and little finger tucked in below, I had to put my right hand into the horse's mouth well down by the grinders, still holding the tongue firmly. Then came Minty's master-stroke, which never failed. A little jerk of the right hand, and the ball slid forward; then the hand was quickly withdrawn, the tongue released, and a sharp slap instantly administered to the soft muzzle. This caused the horse to throw up its head in surprise and to swallow the ball. Minty had been groom to a vet and learnt something about animal medicines; he dispensed some rare concoctions, mixed with black treacle or linseed oil, and they usually worked.

When many cattle were sent from Ireland to be fattened off in our Aberdeenshire byres, where traditionally beasts are tied by the neck, they died like flies. Minty was called in and, saying, 'It's jist the peemony, man,' proceeded to administer his medicines, adding strong mustard plasters to the lung area. These brought tears to the eyes of man and beast, but many of the sick recovered. Minty advised that new arrivals be kept in the open for a while after their long and stifling journey by land, sea and land again from as far away as Co Sligo. He was right; after a period in the fields the cattle could be tied up quite safely for fattening.

He never seemed to receive much money for his work; but loads of straw and swedes would often be seen going to his place. He did all the casualty slaughtering, getting the skins in payment; he was also kept busy killing pigs for home curing. Between the wars the dread 'grass sickness' in horses defeated even

Minty. Then came penicillin, M and B and other modern drugs which made his doctoring unnecessary. He was still called in to calvings and lambings; but he was a little sad at being less in demand. His great physical strength was now declining and, though he still cycled from farm to farm, it was more for the sake of a gossip with neighbours than anything else. He must have been one of the last horse doctors, and farming will be the poorer for his passing.

Socks for an Emperor   by Mary Collier

'Don't go for a minute, love,' said the old lady, 'I want to show you something.' While she rummaged along the cupboard shelves I sat looking about the kitchen. It was a pouring wet day: had it been fine I would not have called on her, for she would have been too busy in her garden to talk. At eighty-nine she still grew flowers, vegetables and fruit, and this morning, but for the rain, would have been hoeing the potatoes. Hers was one of the stockingers' cottages which can still be seen in the Nottingham-shire villages along the Trent valley, and we had been talking about her young days. From my seat I could see into the long room built especially to house the stocking-frames at which her father and five brothers used to work.

She came back with a man's sock of the brightest possible yellow, striped round in purple. 'You see,' she said eagerly, 'it's pure silk. It was one we made for the Kaiser; he liked bright colours. See the little crown here, near the heel? We always had to put a little crown in somewhere.'

'Didn't he like this one?' I asked, turning the gaudy thing over in my hands.

'I expect it was sent back because there was a flaw in it.' She peered at it intently. 'I can't see where it is, but he had to have everything perfect. There were more than three hundred threads on some of the frames, and if one dropped it spoilt the lot. "Half-hose" we used to call socks like this. Sometimes they had clocks woven in—little patterns from the ankle to the calf. My brothers made silk stockings for Queen Victoria, and for the Empress of Austria. She had very small feet, size three in shoes. And they made white silk underwear for King George the Fifth, with his monogram.' The women did the seaming, she told me, standing at their cottage doors chatting to their neighbours. They were never allowed to wash the floors of the rooms in which the frames stood, for fear of rust. Richard Morley, who founded the famous hosiery firm of that name, used to ride out on horseback every week from Nottingham to bring the detailed orders, and no doubt he carried out an inspection at the same time to assure himself that the frames were being kept in good order.

Royalty have worn silk stockings for centuries. Henry VIII wore them, and they are mentioned in a list of the wardrobe of Edward VI. A gift which delighted the first Queen Elizabeth was a pair given to her by Mrs Montague, her silk-woman. She had had them made expressly for Her Majesty, and as they gave so much pleasure she promised that she would at once 'set some

Stockinger's cottage with long window to light the frames

more in hand'. 'Do so,' the Queen is reported to have answered, 'for indeed I like silk stockings so well because they are pleasant, fine and delicate, that henceforth I will wear no more cloth stockings.' She is said to have danced a pair into holes at a ball to show her appreciation of them.

There appears to have been no allusion to woven stockings until the sixteenth century, when an Act of Edward VI spoke of 'knitte hose, knitte petticoats, and knitte gloves'. It is on record that William, Earl of Pembroke (Lord Chamberlain to James I and a Chancellor of Oxford University), was the first English gentleman to wear a pair of home-knitted stockings, which were most likely made of worsted. They were presented to him by William Rider, apprentice to a merchant near London Bridge. This youth had seen a pair brought from Italy, had discovered for himself how they were made, and after some experiment succeeded in copying them.

It was not until 1589 that the stocking-frame was invented, by a curate, William Lee, a native of Woodborough near Nottingham and heir to a large estate. He worked with his frame for about two years, using rough tools and wool from the local sheep. He obtained an audience with Queen Elizabeth, but after wearing silk stockings she was not interested in his woollen ones and refused to grant a patent. Undeterred, he adapted the frame to make silk stockings; but the Queen, fearing that it would throw out of work the many poor people who knitted for a living, again refused a patent.

William and his brother James and nine workmen then went over to France. The MP for Nottingham, Richard Parkyns, had introduced Lee to the French Ambassador, who in turn told his king, Henry IV, about the new invention. The king was interested, promising all sorts of honours and rewards, and all went well for some time. Then Henry was assassinated. William Lee's creditors at once came down on him, seized the machinery and brought an end to his bright career. He died shortly afterwards. James and the workmen came back to England, and after a time a Company of Framework Knitters was established in London. Their arms consisted of a stocking-frame with a clergyman on one side and a woman on the other.

James brought the industry back to his native county, and long after he died a good deal of it was carried on by cottagers in their own homes. Some villages had as many as four hundred frames, but it was not a profitable occupation. The owners charged a high rent for the machines and did not pay well for the output. In 1812 many stockingers were earning only 9s a week, 3s 6d of which was deducted for rent. The Luddite riots occurred about this time. Right up to the present century stockings were regarded as a mark of civilisation, the poor often going barefoot. 'Have you observed the wench in the street? She's scarce any hose or shoes to her feet,' wrote John Walsh in Victorian times, although judging by one of the old cries of London—'Holland stockings, four pairs for a shilling'—they were cheap enough.

The great power looms were evolved on precisely the same principle as in William Lee's original invention, based on a woman's clicking knitting needles. After 1900 the stocking mainly worn was called the 'sanitary black' and was of cotton; not until the early 1920s did it give place to silk and artificial silk. By that time the cottage industry in Nottinghamshire had practically died out, though one or two of the old frame machines have survived. In the village of Hucknall some are still in use, turning out head-scarves, shawls and bed-jackets.

'What happened to your frames?' I asked the old lady.

'Oh, they went back to Morley's after my brothers died. They used to stand there under the windows.' She nodded towards the next room, and I seemed to hear the swishing of the busy machines, a sound characteristic of these midland villages years ago. 'They're long windows, because the workers needed plenty of light. They used to hang water-bottles on the frames to reflect the light on to the needles. There's one, over there.' She pointed to a carafe standing on the dresser. 'It was such fine work, you see', she added as she took the Emperor's yellow sock and put it back in the cupboard.

Tools of a Lace-maker   by Muriel Larner

I have a small collection of lace-bobbins which were all being used at some period during the nineteenth century in the making of pillow-lace, which was then popular. They were usually fashioned from bone or wood, although I have two made of brass. Carved in graceful proportions, from $2\frac{1}{2}$ to $5\frac{1}{2}$in in length, they made attractive tools, light and easy to handle. Fine brass wire and tiny beads were often used as decoration, and a few of the older wooden bobbins were encircled with thin bands of silver.

At one time it was the custom to give lace-bobbins as love tokens, so some have girls' or boys' names tattooed into the stems and coloured, or such messages as 'Love me', 'Marry me quick and love me true' and 'When this you see remember me.' One small bobbin is inscribed 'Fear God.' Another bears the strange question, 'Who is your hatter?' The large bone one on the left of the illustration (see p 51) has on its stem the couplet, 'My hart it cannot rang, I like my choice to well to change.' Only one of my bobbins is dated, and this is of bone, yellow with use; it reads, 'A present from my Aunt Jane 1869'.

The lace-bobbin was finished with a ring of coloured glass beads threaded on wire, and it was customary to add to it buttons or trinkets connected with events in the family: a jet button taken from a dress worn in mourning or a pearl one from a wedding gown. If the sailor of the family brought home a small shell from abroad that, too, was added. A woman often spent most of her life making lace, starting at the age of five at one of the village lace schools and continuing at home on through marriage to old age or death. So it is not surprising that the tools she used also became a record of her life.

My Apprenticeship   by William Gooding

The craftsman peered up the bole of the elm. 'Ay, farmer, I'll take it.' The tree was at Elm Tree Farm, Heathhouse, on a knoll overlooking the flat Somerset moors, intersected by rhines, where every year the river Brue flooded on its slow course to the sea at Highbridge. Thomas Edney, the craftsman, beckoned to me, his fifteen-year-old apprentice: 'See, William? The tree is good—no knots, straight boughs. We'll have it down now.'

Those were peaceful country years. The Second World War was far enough off to be discounted. About us were the heavy dairy farms with substantial Georgian houses. The villages of Mark, Blackford and Wedmore lay like the spokes of a wheel; and the bluish Mendip ridge, with the great Cheddar Gorge, formed a low protecting spine behind us. While other wheelwrights and smiths were installing steam-driven machinery and electricity, Thomas Edney's shop remained an obstinate oasis of hand-craftsmanship. The smithy and workshop, a long span-roofed building, stood only a short distance from the farm. Its double doors, open to all winds and weathers, were like huge abstract canvasses, from the cleanings and primings of many brushes. 'Hurry up, boy! Get this lot clean!' the old man would command. Completely content, I would scrub whorls, noughts, crosses, zigzags and cartoon faces until the brushes were dry of paint.

At the shop the elm trunk was hand-sawn into rough blocks. Holes were then drilled through the centres to allow air to pass into the heart of the wood, to prevent radial cracking. It was my job to pile the blocks in a quiet corner on intersecting slats to dry out for a year. Meanwhile we got on with the turning of matured blocks into wheel-hubs. Every day I scrambled up a rickety ladder to the half-platform in the rafters which housed the 6ft wooden wheel connected by a belt to an ancient lathe below. To a chorus of 'Keep it going, boy. Don't go to sleep up there', Thomas Edney deftly turned the blocks. All around, in neat array, were cleft oak spokes, also shaped by his hand. In the adjoining smithy the bonds were being forged. Bonding day was an exciting occasion with a high accident rate. The red-hot iron bond was taken out to the assembled hub, spokes and ash rim,

'. . . instantly contracted under the hissing steam . . .'

hammered into position round the wheel, then instantly contracted under the hissing steam as buckets of cold water were thrown over it.

The work was mostly seasonal and, as in any other trade, we kept ahead of demand. 'Floods'll be up soon, boy. We'll get half a dozen flat-bottomed boats ready.' These, at £5 apiece, were made from green pliable elm. I would sit sorting out properly angled wood for the ribs. When assembled, the boat was turned keel uppermost and, amid smoke and anvil sparks, we applied pitch to every joint. Later I would have the job of floating the boat out on the water. Sometimes, too, there was the pleasure of lying in the bottom to watch the wild geese go over and, on rare occasions, a pot shot at wild duck with a muzzle-loader.

During the winter we did a great deal of tree-felling. Then the midday meal consisted of a whole loaf of bread, a pound of Cheddar cheese, hacked by Thomas Edney with far less than his usual skill from the body of a truckle, and often a whole shoulder of cold mutton, all washed down with cold tea, as we sat on a fallen tree trunk. On wet or quiet days I turned the old paint-mill

'During the winter . . . tree-felling'

at the back of the shop, pouring red lead, turpentine and linseed oil into it and grinding them smooth. Or, for hours, I would sandpaper panels of the kitchen dressers for which we were noted, until I felt I could truthfully answer the inevitable question: 'Like silk is it, boy? Like silk?' Sometimes I would be set to making iron-ringed hammers of apple wood, popular in the district for smashing coal and peat turves. And the arrival of the eels in the river coincided with the finishing off of the ash handles for five-pronged eel spears made by the smith.

Summer brought a high tide of activity. Rakes, loaders and hand-made wains had to be ready for hay-making. There were cheese presses and butter churns for the milk flush, and apple mills for the cider harvest. The wains, with traditionally blue bodies and red wheels, were made of three woods: oak for the frame, elm for the bodywork and tough ash for the curving front panel. From the local inns and cider-making farms the cry would go up: 'The pummace isn't coming.' Often this meant an enjoyable time away from the shop, sharing the excitement of cider making, while presses were being repaired. For me there was usually a lot of waiting about, and I would be told, 'Help yourself.' Then, sitting on a pile of straw, I would insert a long wheat straw into the trough and, in the warmth and goldness of the day, syphon up sweet unfermented apple juice.

Chief joy of the lunch-hour break was a visit to Mrs Tincknell's shop down the road. Its leaded bow window was almost obliterated by the huge jar of bees' wine for sale at a penny a glass. She had a kind heart for apprentices and schoolboys; and I would return without a care in the world, soothed for the price of threepence by an outsize apple dumpling from the shop oven and two tumblers of alcoholic bees' wine.

Occasionally Thomas Edney went to Bridgwater. He would return with fresh tools, a new leather hide for wheel-washers and half a dozen kegs of paint powder; and his white hair and beard, grown so patriarchal since the previous trip, would have been severely pruned. Every seventh day he laid aside his white carpenter's apron, the ancient paint-decorated hat and the gaming coat with massive pockets. Putting on a black suit and gold chain, he went to the near-by chapel where he was the local preacher. Under pain of royal displeasure I also attended three times on

'Help yourself'

Sunday; and each year I received a book inscribed in the familiar copperplate: 'For regular attendance at Heathhouse Sunday school.' On Monday morning I was asked: 'Did you enjoy my sermon?' 'Yes, sir,' I would reply, upon which we would settle to work. Thomas Edney was an inveterate hummer and whistler of hymn tunes. I would find myself swinging the plane in time to the slow cadence of 'Jesu, Lover of My Soul', only to be shaken by its sharp cessation and the command: 'Smarten up, boy! You'll never be finished.' 'If only he would try "Onward Christian Soldiers" or "Fight the Good Fight",' I complained to the smith, 'I'd get on better.'

When the fifth spring arrived, my apprenticeship years were up. Looking over the moors, I felt I could stay for ever. The floods had gone. The farmer-mariners, who daily paddled their flat-bottomed boats to smithy, stores, inn or chapel, had drawn them up for the dry season. The local boys were at their favourite games of rhine jumping, swimming in the calm Brue and hunting peewits' eggs. But the prospect of learning draughtsmanship at Merchant Venturers in Bristol beckoned. It was time to go.

On the last day, wage in pocket, I took the short road home. At the corner I looked back. Thomas Edney was sitting by his workshop door alone. He had picked up a carborundum stone, and white head bent, was meticulously sharpening the points of a fine hand-saw.

'Thomas Edney was sitting by his workshop door alone'

3 The Shape of Cottages and Their Restoration

Midland Cruck Houses   **by A. J. Woodley**

When the medieval peasant decided to make for himself a more permanent habitation than the little mud hut that had served his forebears, the most plentiful material ready to hand was timber, especially in central and southern England where vast tracts of forest still remained. Hence the 'cruck' house, called 'crog', 'crock' or 'crutch' in some districts. The term 'cruck' in this context meant a wooden fork made from a tree-trunk split in half longitudinally, so that the two matching halves, when placed together, formed an arch. The simplest cruck framework would have been a rough letter 'A', consisting of two pairs of crucks, usually 16ft apart, each strengthened by a tie-beam at head height, and joined by a ridge-pole to support the roof of thatch. The space between crucks was filled with wattle and daub on a subsidiary timber framing. It was the need for more living space that gave rise to the various styles of cruck construction which evolved from the primitive straight-sided 'A', through the curved and Gothic types of arch, to the rare 'elbow' shape as seen at Bournville, made from an angled trunk or from a trunk with a branch. In the next stage the tie-beams were extended outwards to meet vertical wall timbers and carry the horizontal wall-plate from which the rafters sprang. This form can be well traced in the cottage at Wick near Pershore, Worcestershire, but all the cruck houses and barns remaining today show some elaboration of the original primitive 'A' shape. One of the most interesting is that at Didbrook with its straight-sided cruck supplemented by later half-timbering and encased in Cotswold stone. The Barley Mow inn at Clifton Hampden, Oxon, and the Old Thatched Tavern at Cow Honeybourne, Worcestershire, are probably the only remaining examples of cruck inns, both having their crucks wider apart than usual to provide more room on the ground floor. Two other unusual cruck buildings, both in Warwickshire, are at Maxstoke where the crucks reach from ground to apex without a main cross-beam, and Stoneleigh which shows no fewer than six cross-beams set close together. Herefordshire, as one would expect, possesses a wealth of examples, of which the one at Putley is a fine specimen. In Worcestershire there are two wonderful cruck barns at Powick and at Leigh Court, the latter probably the best in England. Many crucks must still remain hidden under later additions and alterations, although it is doubtful whether any true cruck house was built later than the mid-seventeenth century.

My Cottage that was a Barn   by H. E. Bates

I really believe we had been in unfruitful communication with almost every house agent in the south of England. Yet all we wanted was a country cottage, with decent water to drink, reasonable sanitation, and above all a garden, a bit of untouched earth if possible. Nothing elaborate or pretentious. Above all, nothing arty. We were not looking for Tudor manor houses with black yew hedges and old vineries, not because we didn't like these things but because I was a writer and therefore couldn't afford them. I wanted a modest, solid, quiet place in which to live and work and grow flowers.

After two years of search it began to look as if we had asked for a French château or a Spanish castle. Every cottage in England seemed to be either sordid or arty. We visited many, knocking our heads against beams, sniffing cesspools, and getting generally very depressed. 'And why the country?' said my friends. 'In the summer, well, yes. But the winter!' Everything was against us.

But in February 1931 our luck changed, for we came across a Quaker who had some ideas of preserving the countryside and its buildings, and in a casual sort of way he told us that he had amused himself by making a 'bungalow' out of a cowhouse and had further ideas of making a cottage out of an old granary. Did that interest us? It did, but we were dubious. As house-hunters we were getting a bit old in the tooth. Would we like to see it anyway? Well, we didn't mind that. I myself had really got beyond being excited about an old barn.

We inspected, as the house agents say. It was February, it had rained for two days, and the granary stood exactly in the centre of an old farmyard. It was like a derelict ship standing in a sea of mud. It was indeed a sort of ark, the granary itself actually being perched up on two stout stone walls, in order to be high and dry, leaving a sort of half-open cart-shed beneath. The cart-shed was full of what Kentish folk call an old clutter of stuff: cart wheels, beams, buckets, rat-eaten sacks, sheets of corrugated iron. The wind had the true cart-shed iciness. We went upstairs gladly. It was pitch dark, there was a smell of mouldy corn, the wind lifted the roof a bit mournfully. We went downstairs gladly. Really, it wasn't very hopeful. But finally we stood away from the place. And instantly I liked it. It was so square and solid and honest. Its grey stones and chestnut-red tiles were beautifully mottled with bright yellow lichen. It was finely fashioned. Every stone was as sound as when built, the roof came down with the typical Kentish double slope, and above all it faced south and away from the road. I saw myself looking out of windows across the wide field bordered by oaks and horse chestnuts. I measured the thick-ness of the walls—18in. I wondered how much land went with the place? Could I have an acre? What sort of soil was it? What sort of soil! Later I was to trench down to a depth of 4ft without discovering anything but the lightest and loveliest loam that ever any gardener hoped to see.

We admitted it had possibilities. The granary was L-shaped and it would be enough to occupy only the base of the L at first. So we had tentative plans prepared, reckoned the cost, and discovered that for the price of a jerry-built semi-detached monstrosity in a suburban street we could have the cottage we had so vainly been seeking, a place of solid and beautiful workmanship, dry as a granary must be, and planned inside to suit every one of our fads and fancies.

By Easter we had made our decision and the work was in progress. Always remembering that we could one day use the remainder of the L, we planned six good rooms: downstairs a kitchen, a study for myself with east and south windows, and a dining-sitting room 22ft long, with 18ft of window space and an open-hearth fireplace. This room, with its light, its winter warmth and summer coolness, its smooth old pine beams stretching the full length of it, its simple fireplace of warm red brick, has been a joy to us and to all who have seen it. Upstairs we had three bedrooms, all with south-facing dormer windows, and a north bathroom and lavatory. Since the lavatory is of supreme importance, we decided on septic-tank drainage, which functions perfectly. The floors and doors are of polished deal, the doors having simple wooden latches. The floors, being also of great importance, were laid on 18in of concrete. And now the second flood might come and we should sit warm and dry.

The house was finished in a little over six months, a beautiful, neat, snug place that looked as though it had never been a farm-building. And, indeed, it seems odd and half impossible that I am sitting warm and comfortable on a spot where the wind once howled bitterly through the wheels of dung carts and that my books should sit under the beams where birds nested. I do not know how old the place is, only that I have lately come across a beam with 1779 carved upon it, but its history is full of delightful incongruities. Grain was once stored here, and the rats, as old men have told me, came in plagues; and now a baby has been born here and a novel written and Mozart's music sings through the place as often as the wind once did. Yet it has nothing arty-and-crafty about it and as long as I live in it never will have. It is a place for work and living. Grain and words, bread and books —they have always gone together, as any author will tell you. It isn't so long, indeed, since we found some pale yellow grains of wheat still lodged in the crack of an elm-beam under my bookshelves.

The garden needs an article, indeed a whole series of articles, to itself. Meconopsis Baileyi and all kinds of alpines now blossom where there were once forests of prize docks; roses flourish on what was once an old cart track; and today, which is May Day, what was once the farmyard is a blaze of purple and white and lavender and rose and gold.

My Own Cottage   by Adrian Bell

On the one really torrential day of this remarkably fine year we splashed up narrow lanes in search of a farmhouse of which we had particulars. There it stood, turning its back on us across a stack-yard, and looking out over a river valley. It seemed somehow hopeless, starved, pathetic and sightless—only just not derelict. Then the key we had with us didn't fit, or we mistook the door or something. We turned away shaking our heads. Half a mile down the road I said to my wife, 'Perhaps, having come all this way, we ought just to make an effort to get inside the house.' And in that narrow lane somehow I turned the car and we went back. Barley was being stored in the living-room; the brick floors were broken, upstairs they were switchbacks. It seemed more than ever hopeless. Still, there was the view. With the view and just a shred of hope anywhere—? We looked round again. A venerable studded door, an old latch, a grey beam in the wall discovered by fallen plaster; but the fatigue of having to think the place into a habitable state, let alone make it! Only two things we knew about it, the oak was sound, and so was the old tiled roof. It was so dark in there that windy wet March afternoon that we had to look over it by the light of a hurricane lantern. Gradually we got the sense of the odd geography. (It was necessary to go upstairs and down again to reach one part of the house from another.)

I still cannot understand how we came to think anything could be done about it. Its ghosts must have been following us round and pleading for it. The next I remember is that my wife and I were saying to each other, beside the heap of barley, 'It could be done', 'It could be wonderful'—and a rat scuttled across the floor.

We bought the poor old thing, rather in a rush, while the faith was still hot in us. Then we looked at each other as much as to say, 'What have we done?' But now, for better or for worse, we were committed to our heaven on earth. How much safer—from the point of view of personal integrity, I mean—to live in a bungalow and make one's heaven within oneself. But the idea had bitten deep. And because of that we neglected many precautions which our businesslike friends took it for granted we had taken. 'What about death watch beetle?' they cried, and 'Are you sure there's no dry rot?' A battle was waged between friends, on our behalf. Should we have a septic tank or not? Our house, we were told, had been without water, except what was fetched from a spring near by. Then one day a cow had fallen as it were into the earth near the back door, and there, they discovered, was a well which had been hidden for years. I know we ought to have had the water analysed and the well tested and a hundred other things before settling on it. But I have known really astute business men go over a place with a regular army of surveyors, water-diviners, drains inspectors, and so on, and then, when settled in, discover some snag undreamed-of which makes life almost unbearable. Buying an old house is always really an act of faith.

So we spent ourselves and our substance on planning our home, and month by month seeing it slowly realised. We renounced travel in favour of stillness, and freedom for this servitude. And now here it is and we are in it. I look round me and try to see again the house we visited by lantern light that March afternoon. I cannot. The dream has come to life. It is unfinished, of course; it will never be finished. The garden is still a wilderness.

There are two of us: the house is a very real third personality. It is our all in all. It is daring and precarious, I suppose, almost foredoomed, thus to stake one's heart on a heaven on earth. Well, we have attained, even if for a while, our niche. But a thought occurs to me. Perhaps you, stranger, walking across the stack-yard hither (there is still no other approach) would think it as awful as ever it seemed that March afternoon. Perhaps we have but meddled to little purpose and it is still intrinsically as it was. The eye grows in love with familiarity. We see what we want to see. Well, then, after all, our heaven is within us.

Rehabilitation   Anonymous

My dream was the Victorian spinster's cottage with a veranda and a little sitting-room on either side of the front door, a kitchen at the back, four bedrooms above and a shut-in garden. There I would take breath after the crescendo of the last twenty years and enjoy giving the services which the retired professional woman can offer. It must be in that corner of the West Country where I had my roots—for the elderly should not try to establish them-selves in new ground.

After two years' search, when I hoped to be free in a few months, I met the architect whom the agent had found for me and we drove out to a likely cottage. Facing south-east, long in proportion to its width, with walls of cob still faintly flushed with pink and a steep thatched roof, it had a long low window on either side of the door and three windows above. The door opened into a hall, small but not meagre, and opposite us wide stairs led between comely old banisters thickly disfigured with paint. On the right was a room of fair size with a low window-seat cut in the 3ft wall; at the far end a second window, facing west but bricked up, pleaded for the evening sun. The ceiling hung in bags, just clearing our heads. On the left of the entrance door was a quite large room, against one wall of which was the wreck of a second staircase. The murky space beneath it held another bricked-up window and led into a dark doorless cupboard carved out of the thickness of the end wall. Upstairs there was a good bedroom over the sitting-room and another over the kitchen, with the

53

ghostly second stairs leading into it; between them was a third bedroom; and that was all. Outside at the back, on some cobbles, stood a pump with a sink clinging forlornly to it, unconnected to any drainage. Farther back still was the 'useful shed'—a few derelict tiles adhering to a row of decrepit posts. An inspection-pit cover indicated the new drainage system. I felt some doubts when the architect showed no desire to leap up into the roof and test the timbers, and when he satisfied himself about the purity of the water by pumping a little into his hand and tasting it. But he reported favourably on the house, so I bought it for £475 (published Autumn 1952).

An indoor lift-and-force pump, to supply water tanks in the roof, and a water closet were the first essentials. The architect promised to get on with these at once, but weeks went by and it became clear that I must be on the spot to get the work done. When I arrived with a friend in August the builder was still missing. He drifted in at last on his own one day at noon and did two or three hours' work, reducing the neatness of the house to chaos. Two days later he reappeared with a lanky lackadaisical girl, asked for a candle and borrowed some elementary tools. The pair of them visited us at intervals for a fortnight, during which a semi-rotary pump was fixed in the scullery and two 50gal tanks in the roof. Then they disappeared finally it seemed—and as the end of my holiday was near, I appealed to the architect to pay the man off. The pump was easy enough to work, but was certainly not the 'lift-and-force' specified. It produced only a thin trickle of water which was like pea soup. In the end like nearly everything supplied by this builder, it had to be replaced. Meanwhile I found for myself another small man who got on with the job with interest and determination; the sink was placed in the scullery and connected with drains—and that was all I was allowed to do that year.

Throughout weeks of glorious hot sun we had spent every possible moment in the garden. First we cleared a real path to the door. Couch-grass and every other detestable weed were rampant, but on the second day we found that we were exposing cobbles, and when we reached the house we discovered, buried under a foot of earth, a narrow cobbled terrace running round the east and south walls and expanding into a small yard at the back. To clear this completely took several holidays, but it immediately gave dignity to the well-proportioned house.

My next visit was on a day in January, to plant the espalier apples and pears which were to be the background of the herbaceous border. The architect and I then decided to spend that year's £100 on a bath and basin, on reflooring the kitchen, on putting in a hot water boiler and on removing the derelict staircase. He was to send details of a new type of floor at once so that we could apply for the licence, but weeks became months and I could not get the information from him. When a final appeal for immediate action went unanswered I broke away.

A friend recommended in his place an old man in a small way, with whom I jogged out to the house by bus one spring day. He made useful suggestions and promised specifications, but the plan, which went eventually to the rural district council without my seeing it, was inaccurate and obscure. It was rejected and I had to begin again.

This time the chairman of the council, an old family friend, elucidated some of the difficulties, and I journeyed down to meet the district surveyor with a third architect, only to learn that the plan I had discussed with the other two failed to comply with the building by-laws. When we left, my companion shook his bald head: 'I don't know that you've been wise in buying it, you know,' he said. I had seen his own tidy red-brick house in a tidy red-brick row, so I knew our tastes were not akin and replied: 'I know it is not everybody's choice, but it is what I like for myself, and isn't that what matters?' 'I don't know you've been wise,' he repeated. 'Why,' I asked, 'what are you afraid of?' 'Condemnation.' My heart turned over, and I said: 'But how could they? Its perfectly sound and sanitary.' 'You never know nowadays, and those low ceilings,' was his reply.

However, at the end of July the plan was approved and I was free to proceed, if I could show that the water-supply was adequate and pure. Once more I travelled down, this time with a friend. The old architect's face was gloomy. I opened with a cheerful inquiry about a builder. 'I don't know. I've done nothing.' I looked at him with astonishment. 'You were a silly woman ever to buy the place.' Silence reigned. When I replied, 'I think you realise that it is not possible for us to continue to do business unless you take back what you have just said,' he reiterated, 'I said you were a silly woman ever to buy it.' My friend and I rose. I had the plan approved by the council in my hand. 'That belongs to me,' the architect said. 'Give it to me.' We descended the stairs in stunned silence. A few days later I wrote asking for the architect's account, his plan and the council's letter of approval. No answer came. But what the old man did not know was that I had in all innocence taken a tracing of his plan for an interested friend.

During that flying visit I collected a sample of water for a friendly county analyst. Then I had another shock; the water contained every kind of impurity. I did not know then that, if my water supply was deserving of condemnation, so was that of the entire village, and it still is.

When I went down for my next summer holiday, it was with sickening feelings of insecurity. The small builder who had completed the previous year's work for me had most of his men away on other jobs. While I waited to know if he would carry on, I prepared the fruit plot for planting and struggled with the removal of every kind of rubbish. Soon the pile by the gate was far beyond the capacity of a dust cart and I wrote to the district council for salvage collection.

A little man came and arranged for its removal and then, glancing at the inspection pit cover near which he was standing said, 'New drainage I see.' 'Not so very new,' I replied, 'It was here when I bought the house.' 'It has never been inspected by us,' he said, and stooped to lift the cover. The inspection pit was full of sewage. I gazed at him in horrified despair. 'What on earth do

I do now?' 'I don't know,' he said, 'but it will have to be put right, won't it?' He left and I sat down for a few moments' stricken consideration. Then I got out my bicycle. In the village is a big building firm which I had been advised to avoid because of high prices and dilatoriness, but I was now in no case to pick and choose. I explained frankly what had gone before, culminating in that day's horrifying discovery, and the work I hoped to have done then and later.

The builder and his men came next day and have since done all my work. We found that the pipe taking the purified effluent from the septic tank had been placed higher than that bringing in the sewage, which therefore flowed backwards; the soakaway was about the size of a bath and cut in solid clay—ideal for the retention of water in a lake. All this was on my neighbour's land, over which I had an easement. So it seemed that the only solution was to obtain leave to make a second soakaway.

Permission was won—not easily—and the men dealt with that job swiftly. Then the well was pumped out and disinfected. The pump was removed and now a real 'lift-and-force' supplies our needs in five minutes daily, unless we have visitors with urban ideas. The peculiar pea-soup effect disappeared at once.

That autumn the kitchen was transformed. The warm-looking, red cement floor is easy to clean and, in the recess which must have been a big open fireplace, the inefficient little cooker and ghastly old boiler—said to have been the rats' maternity home—were replaced by a new boiler and oil-stove, later succeeded by an electric cooker. The gruesome old stairs went and the dark cavern beneath them to be replaced by a little scullery, lit by reopening the mullioned window over the sink, with a deep china cupboard by the draining board and a large store cupboard opposite. By the back door are the coat and boot cupboards. Upstairs two more reopened windows light the bathroom, which stands where once was the landing. The sagging ceiling of the sitting-room was taken down, revealing fine oak joists, which were scraped, scrubbed and left visible.

In December, worn by twenty years of steadily increasing pressure of work and exhausted by farewells, I arrived on a bleak and icy evening for good. The little house was cold and fireless, choked with the additional furniture which had preceded me, and I was alone. Even so, it offered a welcome and I went to bed peacefully and thankfully.

The next phase could not begin until the start of the new licensing year, but thatching was one of the few industries which had escaped the Government's attentions and I now pursued the elusive craftsman. Not far away lived a master, but his view was that he might do my roof between now and eternity, or again he might not. Also, it was clear from his guess estimate that if he came the cottage would be roofed with gold. A second man called while I was out for a jaunt on a Sunday afternoon and sent a bill (never paid) for thirty shillings for estimating. A third gave me an estimate which I accepted, and said he would begin in a fortnight. For nine months I waited, visiting him every two or three weeks, always to be told that he would be with me in a few days. At last I heard through a farmer friend that he was only keeping me on a string in case the rick thatching which he preferred was short. A fourth man never kept his promise to call, and a fifth said he had too much to do nearer home. Winter was on me again, with a roof which shed large chunks whenever the wind got up, before a friend came to the rescue by lending me his estate thatcher. I bought the reed and learnt that the master craftsman's estimate must have been based on £5 per man-day.

The last permit allowed me to take down the derelict shed and replace it with workshop, fuel-store and garage in elm weatherboarding, roofed from a stack of old red tiles found in the builder's yard, exactly similar to the originals. As soon as the thatching was finished, the external walls were replastered, roughcast and washed to a colour which repeated as nearly as possible the original soft pink.

Now if I look out through my front door, the grass path, narrowing to give an illusion of length, leads to a white weeping rose in a square bed of pink China monthlies. On the right a deep herbaceous border is backed by espalier fruit trees, behind which is a fruit-cage. On the left of the path a narrow rose-bed divides it from a lawn, which is edged on the far side by a long south border of roses and lilies. In front of the dining-embrasure in the kitchen window is a little bee-lawn, protected from the south-west by a low hedge of lonicera. The bed which borders the path round the house gives a continuous joy of colour from the time the grape-hyacinths bloom, followed by tulips, forget-me-nots, polyanthus roses and the giant nepeta, which flowers well into autumn. A low wall of loose stones edges the cobbled yard on which I look as I work in the scullery and is now part of a rock-garden, bounded by pillar roses and bulbs.

By good fortune wealth moved into the farm opposite, and with it came the chance of electricity, so the house now possesses the amenities which should be available for all. It still lacks main water and drainage though both will come in due course. The capital cost, including the purchase price and architects' fees and installation of electricity, has been rather less than £1,100. Two houses of the same size in the neighbourhood—one a jerry-built bungalow standing in a naked parallelogram of ground and the other a substantial brick villa—have been sold since the war for £3,250 each.

The council's houses now cost £1,600 to build, sites and services not included. In spite of all the delays, this house on the brink of dereliction has been turned, at far less cost, into an attractive, comfortable and productive dwelling-place.

Cob and Thatch   by Margaret E. Lowe

It says much for the efficiency of the post office—and much more for the interest, fame and (let us face it) notoriety which surrounds a stranger coming to live in a village some seventeen miles from the coast, the moors and the nearest town—that my first letter was delivered. It was addressed to The Thatched Cottage, Tinker Spinney, Devon. As I looked from my upper window under the deep straw eaves, I saw the village going, roof by roof, down the steep little hill into the wood below: a theme with variations in aurelian, chrome, ochre, russet, silver, sienna and umber. All was thatch from the tousled, grey-green, lichened old wig of John Thorne's the builder's cottage at the crest, to the clipped and combed cap of the hedger and ditcher's linney, newly thatched and shining, celandine yellow, where it caught the early sun among the first young oaks of the wood.

I leant on the sill, sampling the smell of the warm, wet, pastoral west—a nice blend of damp moss, cows, wood-smoke and cream with the astringent tang of the distant sea to give pungency and relieve the sweetness. Turning back into the little room with its yard-thick bulging cob walls, sloping roof-pieces and odd niches and embrasures, my eye went to the big wet patch on the ceiling, to the tell-tale stains on the lime-washed walls. 'A good hat and a good pair of shoes' was the local prescription for a cob cottage that would last down the centuries, and mine had neither.

Even the field and garden walls in these parts were thatched on top and tarred below to protect them against the soft attrition of moisture which, almost daily, not so much rained as hung suspended in the air, collecting in silver beadlets on fine grasses, eyelashes or the hairs of a tweed jacket. Where thatch or tar had been neglected the wall had crumbled and was revealed as nothing but rammed earth—like the houses, earth and straw—but so marvellously contrived as to resist wind and weather for hundreds of years. The post office was known to be sixteenth century and the rest of the village looked about the same vintage.

This matter of the hat and shoes led me straight to the heart of a bitter village feud. The first was the concern of the thatcher, the second of the local builder; and between them deep waters of hatred flowed. This accounted for the decrepit state of the builder's own roof. He could not bring himself to abandon thatch, nor to ask that John Milton (a name common locally) to do it for him. He compromised by pegging tarpaulin over the worst places and staring hard at the roof from time to time, pipe clenched in his teeth, as though he could will a new thatch on it without en-listing the help of the enemy.

I decided to take the bull by the horns: to have both together, give them coffee and tea during morning and afternoon sessions and see what they made of that. My trump card would be the interior decorations, which I was doing myself. I was painting one floor blue, a ceiling aurelian yellow, walls in different shades of slate white, tangerine and nasturtium. Guessing that both men thought in terms of cream, green, beige and kidney brown, I hoped to shock them into awareness of all they had in common and draw them together, even though John Thorne—Jan Tharne to neighbours—did come originally from Hare Monachorum, which had drawn stumps and refused to play Tinker Spinney during a cricket match which Jan Milton was umpiring.

I looked out the thatcher first. In his cottage, a sampler of his craft, I found an elderly woman preparing ' 'e's larnch': bacon, fried bread, toast, honey and 'cut rounds'. Later I discovered that the entire village stopped work about eleven and went home for this substantial meal, and that it was a social solecism to try to see anybody or buy anything at that hour. Dinner was eaten out and about—cold pasties and onions under a hedge—and tea was a large meal of hot pasties and fry at the end of the day. Nobody seemed to have indigestion, but it must have taken generations of conditioning to get them that way.

I left a message for John Milton, and he came round next day. Both his name and calling had led me to expect someone vener-able with, perhaps, a grey patriarchal beard and corduroy trousers tied with straw. John was a smart youngish man with well-cut breeches, shining leggings, a rosy clean-shaven face and the latest thing in cream-and-scarlet motor scooters. He ran over the roof with a pained and expert eye, diagnosed its many ills and priced its reconstruction. It could be patched up, but it would pay me better to have a 'total new 'un'. I agreed, I had fallen in love with the new-baked-loaf appearance of the hedger and ditcher's roof and was determined to have this beauty for myself.

The economics were simple: reed thatch would last twice as long but cost three times as much as wheat straw, and anyway it was wheat straw which shone with that celandine gold in the sun. Its life would be about twenty-five years, John predicted, which seemed long enough for me.

A week later the little back garden was blanketed with straw, and my ginger cat was having the time of his life, crouching behind bales to pounce out on wind-blown straws, racing up and down ladders with fluffed and flying tail like a large red squirrel. He put the ultimate touch of warm colour into a picture composed of the greys, silvers and ochres of the straw, the ivory-washed cottage, the faded blue of John's dungarees and the red of his face. His kit looked impossibly simple for the making of a roof to keep out west-country rain for twenty-five years. In addition to ladders he had an enormous kind of hod to carry the straw, little spiked ladders to stick in the higher parts of the roof, hundreds of bent willow spars and a grooved board with a handle in the middle of its smooth side for thumping the straw into place: that was all. His master tools were his ten fingers, with which he twisted little bundles along under the eaves, smoothed, patted, combed, and moulded his shining pliant medium, until on the last day he came with a great pair of shears to cut the jagged fringe of straws into a neat compact line. This task must have contained for him the crowning satisfaction of every craftsman, the finishing flourish before he stands back from his achievement to 'see that it is good'.

All the time John Thorne was painting the front, drawing the blue-black tarred band at the base with natural judgement and no rule, and I was spreading my joyful gamut of fresh colour on the inside walls. We met for tea, the two Johns stiff-legged as a couple of terriers at first, but unbending over wedges of cake as I gave them liberally that most precious of all village currency, information. I told them where I came from, what I did for a living, how much I had paid for the cottage, what I was going to plant in the garden, why I had come to the west country, what I liked to eat for breakfast. I was sure that they would do the village equivalent of dining out on it for months to come.

The two Johns goggled at my gaudy ceiling and caught one another's eye with a look in which I hoped I detected a little warmth and mutual sympathy, some awareness of their common bond; and again I was reminded of a couple of Irish terriers who always bickered and growled at one another until the day I brought home a cat. Then they stood shoulder to shoulder, staring incredulously at this alien arching thing, and from that day were inseparable. At all events, when after many leisurely west-country working sessions all was done, hat and shoes complete, neat and beautiful, I noticed Jan Milton pushing his smart motor scooter down the cobbled path solely to keep company with Jan Tharne and his truck of tools and ladders.

There are two tailpieces to this story. When the fiercest storm I have ever experienced broke, I was out and about in the village and took refuge under the iron roof of a shed while the rain dropped a solid silver shutter before its open door. The noise of the water hitting that roof was deafening. Cob and thatch, mud and straw, how could they possibly stand against this kind of thing? When I could no longer bear the beating of those words 'cob and thatch' on my mind, I wrapped myself in an inadequate sack and ran the half-mile to my cottage. A waterfall cascaded from the eaves and rushed in fierce bubbles to the ditch; but inside there was not so much as a drop, splash or stain.

Some days later, as I strolled past The Greyhound during its midday session my spine told me that I was the object of attention. I looked up and caught the blue stare of four eyes in two weathered faces. The stare melted into grins as the two Jans raised pint pots in greeting. Cob and thatch had come together again in their natural west-country partnership, and I fully expected to see a new tight roof on the builder's crest cottage before winter frost flung its shawl fringe of icicles along the straw eaves of Tinker Spinney.

Letters to an Evacuee: the cottage   **by An Old Hand**

At the price you paid for it, you have done right in buying the cottage. You will certainly make improvements, and as it is your own you will have the advantage of them if you wish some day to sell. No doubt, at the end of the war, there will be lots of people who, for one reason or another, will want to return to town. So there will be cottages on the market. But it is likely that the price of cottages, like the price of everything else, will have gone up. Your cottage, as well as being a present advantage, will therefore be a reasonably good investment. Carefully improving it to that end will be a pleasant occupation; and you have chosen your district well, for your husband and yourself like it, and the county is not too far from London for him to come down to you.

It is fine that there is a bus route at the end of the lane and that the cottage is on high land and well built. A cottage that is not dry and not well built is hopeless. It is a sink in which it is only too easy to throw away a lot of money to small purpose. Though most cottages look well at the time of year you bought yours, it is November, December, January and February in which they must really be judged. I have often said, Always buy a house in the winter.

It is no small advantage that your cottage is of a village but not in it. To have neighbours near when you are living by yourself with two small children, with your husband in town, is excellent; but a neighbour in a semi-detached cottage or neighbours in cottages across the road would have been too close. You would not have felt that you had the privacy to do just as you like. The little village shop will be useful now and then, though you will find all sorts of tradesmen from the market town calling regularly. Choose among them carefully. For some things you will send to town.

I am glad you have a view. There are people who seem able to do without one. I cannot. Particularly on dark or wet days, a view makes all the difference. It is always refreshing, never two days alike.

And the acre or so of grass accommodation land with a few trees—you are unquestionably in luck's way. That is one of the advantages in buying a dwelling-house which has not been, or was not originally, a labourer's cottage. A labourer's cottage has ordinarily a garden only. A cottage which has been at one time a small farmer's or a retired tradesman's house or a small parsonage —houses in the country go through all sorts of transformations— has usually a bit of land with it. And the cottage is probably better built and has larger and better lighted rooms in it than a labourer's cottage.

Light and dryness are the prime requisites in any dwelling. I remember that the first thing I did with a cottage I once bought was to put in five more windows. Many old dwelling-houses were built under the shadow of the window tax or under the building tradition of the window tax period, and are inadequately lighted for convenience and health.

As to dryness, the fact that you had the cottage inspected makes it pretty certain that the roof was all right. An old roof is often found to be failing. Sometimes the condition is grave, sometimes it is not beyond relatively inexpensive repairs. The architect would also be on the look-out for dry rot. At the worst the situation with dry rot is desperate, for it is almost impossible to get rid of it; few workmen are sufficiently careful. At the best, painstaking applications of the right remedy, at the right time of the year, will gain the mastery.

I am ashamed not to have asked about water. Water of a doubtful character or insufficient in quantity must damn the best cottage—if the sinking of a new and safe well is impossible. To run short of water or not to be sure of the safety of the water-supply is fatal. Plenty of water adds enormously to the comfort, satisfaction and healthiness of life in the country; water under suspicion, water that must be boiled, is expensive and aggravating. It means being deprived of one of the chief blessings of rural existence. Possibly you have piped water or are not too far from the village supply to look forward to having it. If that be so, you no doubt thought of asking elderly residents whether the supply ever ran short.

You have not told me anything about electric light. I hope this is within reach. Even if dear, it is clean, safe, labour-saving, convenient and pleasant. The best oil lamps are a great improvement on what we used to put up with, but lamp filling and trimming is a messy job, and neither that nor looking after lamp glasses can usually be delegated if a good light and a clean lamp are wanted.

Remember that a great many people have set to work before you in improving cottages they have bought in the country. Most of what is necessary is known. Experience has taught a lot. The thing is to act upon it.

By the way, you have not mentioned sanitation. This like the water-supply and the heating of the cottage, has got to be right. Your first and most liberal outlay must be on these. The soundest thing in the end is a small septic tank, and if you don't have central heating there must be one or more perpetual-burning Esse anthracite stoves, with an Ideal or similar boiler for hot water, and—you will never regret it—an Aga or Esse cooker.

But there are all sorts of problems of living in the country besides the problems of health, and of building and equipment. There are the problems of turning the bit of land to the best account with crops and small stock, and, above all, the personal problems, and on these I am inclined to write a few frank words.

4 Cottage Economy

The Triumph of Reuben Mint   **by S. L. Bensusan**
The carrier checked Ebenezer the Second by the side of the
Nutting causeway (or carsey) and looked down with great interest
on Mr Reuben Mint—Ruby to his friends. Mr Mint is small and
dark; he wears a fringe of black whisker that in some mysterious
fashion suggests obstinacy; he has small black eyes, well-nigh
obscured by high cheekbones; he moves with deliberation, almost
with dignity, and is first cousin to Mr Fred Mint, tobacconist and
confectioner on the Hard.

'How do ye howd, Ruby?' demanded the carrier.

'There ain't nowt amiss along o' me, Master Guffin,' replied
Mr Mint.

'I should have heerd tell,' continued the carrier obliquely, 'as
how Ruby bin a' give Master Stump his week, arter twenty years.
An' I no more to do but sez, I will not believe it, ne yet credit it,
ne yet howd that true, till I bin an' see Ruby an' made me own
enquirings. So I looked f'r ye, an' I ain't come acrost ye till a
minit agoo. Then soon as ever I see ye I come up to ye, an' over-
took ye, an' called upon ye to tell me if what folk bin an' towd me
is jest so. There's folk who goo about sayin' th' thing what is not,
bein' they ain't afeared o' hell fire.'

'That's a true word, Brother Guffin, true as if you bin an' said
it in Chapel,' replied Mr Mint.

'But whatever you bin an' done that fower, Ruby,' demanded
the carrier, 'arter all these years? A man don't wanter leave a
place where he should allus have said he liked hisself.'

'That ain't for me to say,' replied Mr Mint, 'ne yet to give particklars. I ain't givin' no informations to nobody. I reckon if anybody come treedin' on a honest man what bin an' worked f'r him this twenty year, he's mos'ly bound to stand up f'r hisself. Don't, there ain't nobody, will not-some-never. An' if you don't say nawthen to nobody, nobody kin say you bin an' said what you never.'

'Do ye come up, Ebenezer,' said the carrier sternly to the horse, as though conscious that all further progress must be physical; 'that's time we bin an' jubbed along. Fare thee well, friend,' he added to Mr Reuben Mint. 'But,' he added still more sternly, 'that don't do to be too stand-offish in this world, more especial like to them what you set under reg'lar come Sundays.'

'There's things in this here world we ain't intended to know about,' declared Mrs Wospottle, the wise woman, mysteriously when old Miss Thake, who does not lack courage, asked her what she made of Mr Mint's case. 'There's folk,' she added, as though to shed a little light on the case, 'what do things bein' they can't help theirselves like, an' Ruby Mint is same as a warm man. He ain't a man what got to goo here, there an' everywhere without he want he should.'

One might go beyond all cryptic utterance and say that Mr Mint is very warm indeed, if personal property sends up temperature. He owns his cottage and half an acre of garden and orchard, both well tended. Furthermore he owns two productive Large White sows, a small apiary and a pen of chickens that spend all their spare time laying eggs, while in Mrs Mint he has a helpmate who can clean, cook, pickle, preserve, bake and keep her temper; nobody has ever charged Charity Mint with clanjanderin'. While there is wonderment, it is admitted by all discerning men that Mr Ruby Mint 'ain't behowden any to that Master Stump', and that if he is so disposed he can 'goo on a loose leg'.

So it befell that on a Friday night Mr Mint left Armiger's, and on the following Monday evening Mr Stump who farms it, surveying the day's work of his successor at the plough, found fault.

Later he wanted a little mole-draining in the Five Acre and discovered that nobody would undertake it. He sent a score of pigs to Market Waldron and they fell to Mr Caplin at that gentleman's own price.

'That's some lucky,' said Mr Caplin to a henchman, 'Jerry Stump got riddy o' that man Mint. He'd ha' run th' stuff up rather than let a honest man come by it. I count he's took th' food outer me mouth many's th' time. I'd ha' gi'e a couple o' pun to th' man who could tell me Ruby Mint bin an' slipped his wind.'

'I feel the miss o' Ruby Mint,' declared Mr Stump later on to his better half over the ample tea-table. 'He ain't bin gone a month an' I count he's cost me ten pun.'

'You should ha' let him have th' owd fowl 'us,' said Mrs Stump placidly.

'That's a piece,' cried her husband greatly disturbed. 'Why, that was you what towd me not to. I couldn't make me mind like, till you bin an' made it up for me.'

'I wore wrong,' suggested Mrs Stump. 'We don't all know everything in this world; we gotter find out. I gotter allow I made a mistake.'

'Jetty Vange ain't done nawthen with it yet,' mused Mr Stump aloud.

'He'll ast ye ten-shilling profit, 'lay,' prophesied Mrs Stump, who has a Cassandra strain in her make-up, and she was right. Mr Vange, who had not ceased to listen to criticism of his purchase from gossips declaring that the fowl-house took up too much room in his small garden, did demand a ten-shilling profit, but in return for it helped Mr Stump to pack the fowl-house on the van and promised not to talk. As he never talks without effort, the concession was easy, but it atoned to Mr Stump for money lost.

'I count,' suggested Mr Stump looking over the hedge at his old-time worker now busy in his garden, 'you'd better come back to mine, Ruby Mint. You ain't like yourself any, since you ain't got nawthen to do. I lay me life you can't be happy without a job o' real work.'

'Soon as ever I bin an' dug me garden over,' explained Mr Mint to the stout agricultural implement in his hand, speaking to it without emotion, 'I'm gooin' to build meself a fowl 'us an' it's gooin' to be a headpiece. I'm gooin' to see Ben Cant Saturd'y arternoon about th' wood.'

'There ain't no need, Ruby Mint,' interposed Mr Stump. 'You kin have th' fowl 'us out o' me Fower Acre.'

'I should hear tell,' said Mr Mint to the fork, 'as how Master Stump bin an' sold it to Jetty Vange, 'cause he bin an' offered him twenty-five shillin' stiddy a pound, time he should say he wanted to git riddy of it.'

'That's come back,' explained the farmer shortly. 'You kin have it f'r y'r pound, same as you offered me.'

'That on't sinify nawthen to me now,' Mr Mint explained a little forgetfully to the fork, 'bein' Bob Gaymer bin an' spoke f'r me Rhode Islan's what I wanted it fower. Nine pullets an' a masterful gret ole fowl. I doubt,' he continued, more forgetfully still, 'if I wanted him to give 'em up, arter he spoke f'r 'em an' all, that'd cost me ten shillin', bein' I give him me word, an' everybody gotter allow I gotter good charater an' riteforward.'

'You kin have the owd hen 'us f'r ten, Ruby Mint,' cried Mr Stump with emotion.

'D'ye think that'd be brought up here f'r that?' inquired Mr Mint of the fork.

'That'll be brought right inter y'r yard, Ruby Mint, an' set up where you want it,' said Mr Stump mopping an anguished brow.

'I kin come back to ye o' Monday mornin', Master, if so be ye want me.' Mr Mint found himself at long last looking at Mr Stump and addressing him without the aid of an intermediary.

'You'll git th' owd house tonight, an' I'll stop th' ten shillins outer y'r money come th' Friday,' replied Mr Stump.

'I count you mean five shillin' each o' two Fridays, Master,' said Mr Mint.

'You're double cunnin' to my thinkin', Ruby Mint,' growled Mr Stump, 'but there I ain't gooin' to fall out along o' ye arter twenty year. I've felt th' miss o' ye an' that's th' truth.'

Men rubbed their eyes. Men used their tongues. Women did the same. But Mr Vange has kept his word, Mr Stump is naturally reticent, Mr Mint invariably so.

'If I bin an' let Ruby Mint have th' owd fowl 'us right away,' said Mr Stump ruefully, 'I count I'd ha' bin fifteen pound in pocket.'

'An' if he hadn't come back, that might ha' bin tharty be now, what you'd ha' bin an' lost,' said Mrs Stump for his consolation. She is one of those good wives who always look on the bright side of things.

Housekeeping in a Cottage   by Sylvia Townsend Warner

'I have a country cottage' may mean the possession of anything from a bungalow to a small manor house, from a semi-detached villa to a reed-thatched, old-oaked architect's fancy, plumbed within and half-timbered without. My cottage has four rooms, and would let, unfurnished, at the usual local rental of 2s to 2s 6d a week (April 1933). It is neither picturesque nor convenient. But it is a freehold, and stands in a small garden, and its price was £90 only.

When I bought it its water-supply consisted of a water-butt and an understanding that the tenant might fetch water from a well farther up the road. Fortunately, its back kitchen, being a lean-to, had a roof sufficiently lofty to allow of a small tank being fitted indoors, collecting the rain-water off the slate roof. To this I added a small sink, draining into a sump in the garden; and while heaven permits (and in this convenient climate heaven generally does) this allows me a water-supply for kitchen purposes.

Only those who have had to carry water into the house and out again can appreciate the beatitude of a tap, and a run-away.

I have, when I choose, constant hot water also, for the lofty back kitchen had a copper in it. There is a general idea that a copper is useful only on washing day or for boiling Christmas puddings. This is a great mistake. A copper is most valuable in solving two great problems of village living: how to have enough hot water, and how to dispose of rubbish. To work well, it must be kindled like a fire; with sticks, cinders, and enough coal to raise the water almost to boiling point. After this, and fifteen to twenty minutes should be long enough, it can be fed with the surprising quantity of papery rubbish which accumulates in any present-day household; and with a little more attention, and a few handfuls of cinders, the water will remain hot all day. A copper will burn almost anything, it will even calcine tins; but it is a waste to feed it with vegetable rubbish, which can be rendered into garden manure.

Like most village people I cook on oil, with a 12gal oil drum replenished by the monthly van. As the copper is one mainstay, the stock-pot is another. With a stock-pot I can snap my fingers at tinned soups and meat extracts. At its richest, it gives me a consommée; at its most exhausted, the basis of a mulligatawny. And in its way it is as useful as the copper at engulfing fragments. But, people say, a stock-pot, unless constantly re-boiled, is apt to go sour. It will, if, when taken from the fire, the lid is left on and the steam allowed to drip back; it may, if vegetables are put with the bones and meat trimmings. But it is not necessary to add vegetables; a bouquet of herbs will give it an aroma, and if vegetable stock be needed, it is far better made of vegetables alone.

After buying her stock-pot (and let it be of stout aluminium, not the traditional iron tank so unwieldy and slow to boil) the cottage cook will be well advised to stock a herb-bed, the nearer the kitchen door the better. It should contain at least a dozen herbs: sage, green and purple, mint, marjoram, tansy, chives, parsley, thyme, common and lemon-scented, tarragon, hyssop, basil, savory, southernwood, rosemary and balm. Nasturtium leaves and seeds are admirable in their season, fennel is liked by many, and there may be a use for rue, though I must say I have not found it. Having grown these herbs, and they will all grow as obligingly as weeds, she must study their flavours, learn to compound them, and learn, above all, not to use too many of them at once. Such combinations as chives and nasturtiums, tansy and balm, thyme and southernwood, are as exquisite as the usual mess of mixed herbs is dreary.

From the kitchen door it should be easy to keep an eye on the garden to avoid that wasteful tragedy, the too-well-matured vegetable. A broad bean kept till its green jerkin has turned to a fawn spongebag is a broad bean misunderstood. Bullet-like peas, long, tough, hairy runner beans, harvest-festival marrows—those who live in towns or placate a gardener must put up with these; but the cottage cook, if she grows her own vegetables, need not submit to such odious longevities. She must pounce on the innocents; nature will always see to it that there are enough sexagenarians.

A Wooden Harvest   by Peter Rosser

Old men who were boys here in Hampshire remember bavins, those bundles of twigs which were lit inside the old brick ovens. After the burnt ash had been raked out, the plump bread-dough was put in. For household kindling today, 'gas-pokers is yer bavins,' the woodcutter reckoned; 'nothing cut now smaller 'n pea-sticks.' All about him were the bundles of hazel; and the stools from which he had cut them stood short to the ground, like sharp yellow teeth.

'These longs is bean-sticks—twenties, they calls 'em. Fetch about six shillin' a bundle in the market. That's around three an' threepence here on the ground when they comes fer 'em theirselves from London. About eight-year growth, them. Then there's yer fifties an' seventy-fives, mostly fer the Staffordshire pots. Yer hundreds, fer pea-sticks, you leaves twiggy, the others you trims into poles, like. They still reckon the best thing fer pots in Staffordshire is a hazel basket. Don't never matter how much those old goods-wagons creak an' shudder, yer hazel basket creaks an' shudders to it, like. You won't lose a single pot in one o' them baskets. Never found anythin' to beat 'em, not at the price, an' I don't reckon they will, 'cause it's nature, see. You can't never beat nature, not at the price. Like my withs: some bundles up with wire, but what are you goin' to do with a thousand bits o' wire? But you can burn yer withs.'

He took up a wand of hazel about as thick as a little finger and, setting the butt under his foot, worked four or five clockwise twists into it. Then he bent over about a foot of the tip and twisted that round the stem in the same direction. The loop stayed.

'I could do you a with like that as 'ud take a ton pull, they reckon. But the thick 'uns is terrible on yer hands. An' if there's any frost in the with, it don't twist at all—just snaps, like. No good to this job at all is frost. Snap yer bill-hook will a good frost. Can't buy a bill-hook like mine today. Made local from an old blacksmith's rasp an' keeps an edge like a razor all day. But if 'twere frosty today I wouldn't be usin' it, not on yer life. Get frost in that an'—snap like a biscuit. Today it's just windy. Always windy up here on this brow. I generally has a fire, but I'll tell you somethin' I've noticed an' you haven't: fire's like water fer runnin' downhill. Light one up there, an' within the hour yer fire's down here. Yes, you'd think 'twere the set o' the wind but I've watched, it's the slope.'

The woodcutter liked working up here on his own and being his own gaffer. There was always plenty to see, he said.

'I was sittin' with me thermos, an' over there come a fox to sit on the edge o' the spinney. Never saw me, an' I made a good study of him, just sittin' there wrinklin' his nose a bit in the sunshine. Blow me, come tea-time I went fer me thermos an' there he was, up on the very last joint of his hind legs, tall as he could make, havin' a good study at me. Another day I was comin' through the ride on me way here, an' there was a fox cub dead. That night, goin' home, I saw its mother, I reckon, crossin' the field with the dead cub in her mouth, an' all the way across, rooks was dive-bombin' 'em. There's always somethin' to see, if you've got eyes.'

'Course, it isn't my regular job. I only does this in between, like.'

'In between what?'

'Well, like, between one job an' another. I can make about twenty twenties a day—cut, trim, count, with up. I've done twenty-eight one day, but that's tryin' to kill all yer own enthusiasm, like.'

Declining Croftlands   by Audrey B. Holmes

The definition of a croft is given by a frustrated crofter as 'a small piece of land surrounded by regulations'. It is a fair assessment where crofting exists under an array of complications, natural, traditional and legislative, brooded over by various commissioners, assessors and other officials. A story is told of an elderly crofter on Skye who, while chatting with a visitor, complained of the increasing amount of smoke on the island. The visitor looked in astonishment at the pastoral scene around him. 'Smoke?' he asked. 'What smoke?' The old man replied firmly: 'There iss too much smoke; and it iss from the cars of all these Government officials it iss coming.' But crofting, despite the attentions of these gentlemen, still languishes. The Crofters Commission set up in 1955 is regarded with cynicism; and its hand on the patient's brow, sincere and well-meaning though it may be, has provided no effective cure.

To be more precise, a croft usually is a land holding of not more than 75 acres, or with an annual rent not exceeding £50, situated in one of the seven crofting counties of Argyll, Inverness, Ross and Cromarty, Sutherland, Caithness, Orkney and Zetland, which include a wide variety of ground from the rich land in the east to the peat and bare rock of the west. There are 19,670 crofts, and only 2,000 are of more than 50 acres. In the West Highlands and Islands the majority are under 10 and frequently between 3 and 5 acres, although the minimum self-supporting size today is estimated at 20 acres with good hill grazing.

Each croft has a souming. This specifies the number and kind of stock a crofter is permitted to place on the common grazing attached to the 'township'. It may be as small as two cows and followers, with perhaps a horse, or even half a horse, which may be interchangeable with a certain number of other stock; or it may be three, thirty or more sheep, as pasture, arable and good fortune go. As may be imagined, economic pressure can be heavy on the holders of such small plots of land, though conditions vary widely. Climate and soil may differ even from one glen to the next and from one island to another, as may the methods of crofting.

Most crofts are gathered in townships—communities whose minimum size may depend on the supply of a crew for a boat. A few are scattered separately over the land. Many are fenced in, but others still work on the open system where the croft land, even if fenced, is made available for all the stock to graze between October and March. The individual who improves his ground then finds the township animals rushing on to it as soon as the gate is opened. The land worked may be a small patch among the rocks, the soil scraped into ridges on which potatoes can be planted; or fields reclaimed long ago from the heather. It may be on the slope of a hill barely workable by machinery, on flat machair land (grass over shell sand) or in a fertile and sheltered spot, like the famous Inverewe gardens in Wester Ross, but only a few miles from land that is bleak and swept by salt-laden winds. Subsidiary employment, scarce but essential, may range from fishing, weaving, forestry and road-making to the jobs of sexton, postman and pier-master. Tourism benefits many, but it may also require that the crofter and his family sleep on the floor of their small cottage, or live in a shed while it is let. It makes life hard for the woman who also helps on the croft. Some doubt if tourism and crofting do go well together.

Scraping soil into ridges before planting potatoes

Those who wield most power over crofters are the Crofters Commission, the Land Court and the landlord. The Scottish Land Court has always been accepted as a thoroughly impartial body whose decisions, following inquiries on the spot, are respected. Unfortunately some of the Court's powers passed to the new Crofters Commission; and as an administrative body it soon came to be viewed in a less favourable light. The Commission's duties included those of compiling a register of crofts, controlling letting, dispossessing absentee crofters, reorganising townships, administering agricultural and other grants, and so on; but it has

77

had no power to tackle the urgent social problems or to attempt land development. Although legislation this year restored to the Land Court its lost functions, it has not widened the scope of the Commission. The latter does have some power during reorganisation, when land is re-allocated and amalgamated, to bring into

A fisherman's croft

crofting use non-crofting land in the vicinity of a township; but it has achieved that in only one of eight schemes. This is far from being the vigorous policy of land settlement many advocate as essential for these emptying districts. In 1892 a Royal Commission assessed the amount of land suitable for settlement at 1,783,000 acres, and of this only approximately 23 per cent has been used.

But the question of land settlement and sporting estates is a spiky thistle. Certainly the powers of landowners, the majority of whom are absentee, can be unfortunate. There is the landlord whose estate includes a village, and whose conditions of let prevent the sale of goods which compete with those in his own store; when local competition introduced travelling vans, he refused them garage space on his land. Another will not permit an access road to cross a corner of estate land to a neighbouring crofting community. Others, it was asserted in Parliament, may deliberately avoid letting out vacant crofts and thereafter resume the land; the croft house sold or let for holiday purposes fetches a good sum, whereas the crofter pays rent for the land only, being responsible for providing and maintaining on his croft, which is heritable, his own house, sheds, etc., for which he will receive compensation if he leaves. Not all landowners are as selfish, yet these instances do not stand alone. The principal considerations, however, are not individual rights or wrongs, but their combined effect on the counties from which 15,186 people have migrated in the past ten years.

The population of the crofting counties today is 277,716, of which a lesser part is urban. In the landward areas the remaining 177,292 people face considerable social difficulties. Doctors and hospitals may be many hours away by sea or air. Education is becoming increasingly centralised and breaking up the close-knit family life of the Gael. Children from twelve years of age must often live away in hostels or lodgings, and boat time-tables may permit them to return home for only a few hours on a Saturday. There are few buses on the roads, and some places are without public transport by either land or sea. Some crofts have no access for vehicles at all, and in many other areas the roads are very rough. Markets for all goods are far away, and freight charges show heavily on every item in or out.

On the land there has been for generations a crippling lack of capital with which to effect improvements and buy machinery. There is also a lack of modern agricultural knowledge; and as the land has deteriorated, so hopelessness has grown. The young and ambitious who have gone, not all by desire but some by necessity alone, have left an ageing population who become physically unable to work the land. The eagerness of the younger men who remain may be frustrated in communal effort by the age or pessimism of fellow crofters, and hampered by the restrictions of official bodies.

Much has been blamed on the crofters themselves. They have

been variously accused of being lazy, suspicious, lacking in initiative and unwilling to help themselves. These accusations, while no doubt as true of some individuals here as everywhere else, are perhaps heard most often from people without intimate understanding of crofting conditions or of human beings who for generations have experienced depression and extreme poverty and who, through long endurance of this state, are unable to surmount the difficulties unaided. Many have lost heart undoubtedly. What surprises is the number who still struggle along for so little reward; but as one crofter has said, 'If I was not born there and the very dust of the place dear to me, I would quit tomorrow.'

To understand all this one must realise first that, in this north-west corner of Britain, there still exists a culture whose social philosophy is not that of our own commercial society. The Gaelic communities in the Hebrides and parts of the north-west mainland are one of the oldest cultures remaining in Europe, possessing the same roots as the Irish Gaeltacht, with whom they considered themselves, up to the seventeenth century, to be one people. Gaelic literature preserves a record of society at a more archaic stage of development than is obtainable from any other literature in Europe apart from Latin and Greek; while the oral tradition—the folk tales and historical accounts from ancient times still on the lips of people among the islands—have their counterpart in other countries only in manuscript form. These links form a still viable connection to a remote past; and it may then be less surprising that more recent history should also be alive in Highland memories and capable of influencing people's outlook today.

Crofting has had a turbulent history—often one of long struggle in face of the repressive or indifferent attitudes of early Governments, from the persecution of the patriarchal clan system, which gave the Gaels their leaders, to the times of Jacobite rebellion and the firing of townships, cottages and crops by Government troops. There followed the forfeiture of clan estates, disintegration of that social system, some voluntary migration and then the disastrous replacement of people by sheep. The last of these Highland Clearances, in which people were driven from their homes, away from the land they or their forebears had reclaimed, occurred as recently as the middle of the nineteenth century. With the assistance of troops dispossessions were often brutally carried out; even the aged and the sick were mercilessly ejected, their cottages and furniture being burned as they left. And the influence of these clearances is not gone; the evictions are still bitterly termed 'barefaced stealing'. The remaining crofts stood on the land unwanted for sheep; and it is on this same poor soil, on land particularly hard and unrewarding to work, that many crofts remain today.

The small tenants who survived the clearances and crowded on to the available land were wretched in poverty. Years of famine arrived, unrelieved by Government assistance, when people scratched for food along the beaches. They were at the mercy of the estate factors, liable to eviction at a whim, often under extreme pressure, which led to rioting. It was not until the Crofters Act of 1886, which followed the Napier Commission's

'Their cottages and furniture being burned as they left'

report published three years earlier, that security of tenure and fair rents were established. The commission recognised that the majority of crofters could not earn their living from land alone, but effect was given to only a few of its recommendations. Since then legislation has dealt only with the land. The social problem as a whole has not been tackled yet.

This then is the background to crofting. It is a history whose offspring are mistrust and cynicism in an exhausted population. In these quiet places tradition dies slowly, and the warning can still be heard to watch how you speak with so-and-so who, as 'a man from the Government', should be greeted with caution. That this attitude leads to administrative difficulties is probably true, but understandable; yet a policy of explanation and 'public relations' might overcome it. It is only one of the facets of the Celtic character which also give us an individual, humorous and extremely likeable people with a respect for education, a taste for literature and music, and in some respects a sensitiveness and courtesy towards others which may extend to extremes; the guest who mis-states a fact may remain uncorrected, or a speech of unpopular content be applauded in appreciation of a good delivery.

If there is a lack of leadership from within, it is partly because this is still a comparatively classless society, composed of people possessing the same broad range of skills. A crofter usually is a man of considerable intelligence and ability, who must complete for himself the variety of tasks a remote environment lays on him; they may include building his house with his own hands, as many do. He is accustomed to think for himself in daily tasks, and to attend one of his vigorous meetings is to listen to a surge of individual ideas which makes obvious the need for a leader who can channel these tributaries into one river. It has been agreed by commissions and scientific investigators that outside assistance is required; the swimmer with cramp cannot achieve his own rescue.

That possible remedies exist can be seen in such studies as

F. Fraser Darling's 'West Highland Survey' and Adam Collier's 'The Crofting Problem'. There are also the examples of other countries. In Eire industry is now being attracted successfully from abroad by the offer of non-repayable grants and considerable tax concessions; and in the Netherlands the legal basis of

Sheep in place of people

land redistribution schemes was gradually changed to include land improvement with planned development of roads, drainage, land levelling and cultivation. Many believe firmly that with a well-considered policy our own land and its people could be saved from further decline, not overnight but slowly.

Even in the present gloom bright spots indicate potentialities. Advisers from agricultural colleges initiated both bulb growing in the Hebrides and the dramatic reseeding of moorland on the island of Lewis, achieved by the co-operation of crofters in whole townships, despite delays caused by lack of capital. The first lobster-marketing organisation in Shetland does booming business, and the cash value of the lobsters which pour in from crofter-fishermen to the storage tanks at Scalloway rose from £7,143 in 1954 to £60,000 in 1960. In South Uist a marketing scheme for eggs thrives. In Stornoway, Lewis, the advent of a deep-freeze and canning factory for shellfish has brought inquiries to the Highland Fund—a non-profit-making organisation which provides loans to crofters and others from funds publicly subscribed—for capital to purchase boats and outboard motors. Then J. M. Rollo has initiated small industries at Easdale, Wick, Kinloch Rannoch and Inverasdale. At Inverasdale in Wester Ross, where five crofters are employed, he also introduced his own improvement scheme, which has resulted in a township no longer in decline, with crofts well kept and school attendance figures beginning to rise again. Near Fort William, after extensive land drainage, J. W. Hobbs established a cattle ranch on what had been a peat bog.

Of considerable importance may be the formation of a Council of Social Service on the island of Mull. At the time of writing (Winter 1961) the Council is due to meet the representatives of departments, commissions and boards and others in the hope of persuading authority to adopt a plan for the rehabilitation of the island; a development scheme is envisaged for communications, social services, agriculture, small industry and weaving. It may be that Mull, with a large number of incomers who have been in the Services, is better equipped to lift herself from the morass of decline than most communities; but this lead is urgently required. Will it be followed elsewhere?

Where, in place of mere reallocation of strips of land, are the agricultural and marketing schemes to place before the crofters of each area, showing them how best their district might be developed, where and how both old and new products might be marketed, and giving them generous guidance and aid to equip and regenerate their land? Where is the research unit to

Summer milking

work on a pilot scheme of this kind? Or the development board composed of both business men and agriculturists, with money and authority to bring their plans to fruition? In places such as Kenya and Malaya the commercial Colonial Development Corporation assists local government to develop smallholder schemes adjacent to nucleus estates, which supply them with skilled guidance, centralised processing facilities and co-operative marketing. This is the kind of help which could be of use in the crofting counties. From their remote districts crofters cannot easily 'develop markets' in a world of business from which they have been apart for a long time. Yet the basic fact is that much of this part of Britain is under-developed. We need visionary leadership; and there are a few men who, given the opportunity and resources, could provide it.

85

Well Wrapped Up   by Stephen Ryan

The Ulster countrywoman was describing the attire of her rheumaticky old mother, bedridden for sixteen years. 'Furst iv all she hess hurr flannenette shimee, then she hess hurr stockin's, then she hess hurr cambinations, then she hess hurr red flannen drawers, then she hess hurr corsets, lined wi' flannen, then she hess hurr nightgown on the top iv that, then she hess the blouse I gat made for hurr that's too tight in the armholes, then she hess hurr pattycoat, then she hess the black kerdigan I bought hurr, then she hess the new grey kerdigan our Willie bought hurr, then she hess hurr two wee shawls an' a skirt roun' hurr showlders an' annythin' else she kin gather up. Then she hess four feather pillas, a wee cooshion at this side an' an owl coat in a bunnel at the other side, hurr stick in bed wi' hurr an' a wee tin box she keeps hurr wee nigmanoys in. An' she lies there an' bombardeers us from the bed mornin', noon an' night.'

The Little Laundry Maids
by Amoret and Christopher Scott

When we acquired our sixteenth-century half-timbered cottage in Worcestershire, our predecessors showed us the foundations of a large building in the paddock behind the house, and a small leather-covered book which had been passed on to them by the previous owners. The site had been occupied by a laundry which was run as a training school for young girls from local institutions. The book had been used by the matron of the establishment, who lived with her staff in our cottage, to record the advent, progress and subsequent fate of each of her charges. Their average age on arrival was about twelve, though in 1888 one, Edith Crane, was admitted at the age of seven. All had originally been taken into institutions with a background of broken homes: dead, crippled, insane or worthless parents. A common formula is 'Father dead, mother deserted her.'

From 1870 until 1925, when the home was finally closed, there is a complete record of the running of the laundry. The girls washed all the linen of the great house which patronised it, and neighbouring houses could have their washing done at reasonable prices. In 1905 damask table-cloths up to 3yd long were laundered for 6d; nightdresses cost 8d, 9d or 1s 6d depending on whether they were white, flannel or silk.

There seems no doubt that the establishment was well and efficiently run according to the somewhat stringent principles of the time and circumstances. It was inspected annually, and there were regular visits by the chairmen of the unions from which the girls came. While the reports inscribed in the book are uniformly complimentary, one cannot avoid the picture of the pathetic twelve-year-olds who lived and worked there, pummelling the huge sheets and tablecloths in an atmosphere of steam for most of the hours of daylight (and a good many dark ones in winter) and packed off to bed in the long bare dormitories. In some of their reports the inspectors do remark that the girls seemed to be working over-long hours. Their pleasures were obviously few. Country dancing was allowed once a week; those who could sing at all attended choir practice, and all were scrubbed for church, where attendance was compulsory three times on Sunday.

If the girls had a thin time of it, the matron's patience must often have been sorely tried. 'Five girls were so rude to Mrs Kitching that they were punished by having no pocket-money and no eggs for breakfast. They object to doing their work over again when not properly done.' 'Florence Ratcliffe's character not very satisfactory. She cannot get up in the morning.' 'Mary has to remain out of the laundry, she is so naughty.' One particularly unfortunate affair involved Trumper, the boiler man and only male in the establishment, Mrs Kitching the laundry matron and Ethel Anderson, one of the girls:

> 25th July, 1893: Trumper has been very troublesome this week in putting the girls up to mischief and sauciness. He is also a great deal to familiar with them, especially Ethel Anderson.
> 28th July: Matron has had a serious talk with Ethel. She had,

however, been very impudent to Mrs Kitching and was sent to bed in consequence.

4th August: Trumper has been given notice to leave, chiefly on account of the girls.

It must be added, however, that the rebellious Ethel went on to make good and was finally placed as housemaid in an unknown mansion, whence favourable reports were received.

Not all of the girls survived the rigours of the laundry, and even the first laundry matron in 1871 became 'mentally affected'; eventually she drowned herself. Several girls are recorded as being untrainable and were returned to the institutions from which they came. One complete page of the book contains a name, date of arrival and the laconic statement, 'Ran away'.

When they had made their own 'trousseaux', an essential part of which were two pairs of black knitted stockings, most of the girls were placed in the great houses of England at wages ranging, in the 1870s, from £12 a year for a fifth laundry maid to £14 for a second, plus 2s 6d a week beer money. Those not sturdy enough to do laundry work were found other forms of domestic employment at reduced rates: in 1874 Caroline Hall was sent out as an under-kitchenmaid at the wage of £7 a year—and no beer money.

The home must have been a blessing to the governors of local institutions, which were always overflowing with the debris of unhappy households. Although the girls had a hard life they did at least reap the benefit of decent occupations in an age when unemployment was the rule rather than the exception. The foundations of the laundry will probably remain in the paddock for all time, for they go deep into the local soil.

5 Church and Verse, Schoolbooks and Handbells

Sing Joyfully   **by Bridget Pears**

The small choir—offshoot of a bigger choral society—meets irregularly, being summoned only when a specific performance is in view. The final practice starts with a brief chat about the condition of our throats. Solicitously we inquire after laryngitis, relaxed throats and catarrh, and ask if last week's cold has departed. We are very suspicious of a snuffling sneezer who saturates countless tissues yet blandly assures us that she is 'not infectious now'.

The baton calls us to attention; we take deep breaths and begin work. Soon someone is caught whispering and there is an unpleasant pause while the culprit is shamed into silence. One of our number is heavily pregnant and can frequently be detected desperately gasping for breath, causing our choirmaster to glare disapprovingly and announce that 'people' are snatching breaths all over the place.

Work progresses and we all grow weary. Then violent discussion breaks out over Latin pronunciation, good for a ten-minute breather if handled astutely. The battle is between the scholars and the musicians; the former—mere archaic purists—favouring classical pronunciation, with the latter pressing the claims of the Italianate form. Happily for our vocal chords the musicians are in the majority and sway the conductor; it is to be 'exchellsis' and not 'exkellsis'. Nobody mentions 'exsellsis'.

Refreshed by this spirited interlude, we return to our singing and are bullied, cajoled and constantly exhorted to do ever better. Finally, with aching throats and deflated lungs, we reach the end of the final bar and stagger uncertainly into our seats, nearing the limits of exhaustion. We shall not meet again till the performance.

It will be our first visit to St Anonymous and we want a preview on essentials. Will it be well-heated or not? Is the vicar likely to disapprove of low necks, or no sleeves, or short skirts, or all three? Our questions answered, we mentally select the little-black-dress best suited to present requirements; the Lower the Church, the higher the neck proves a sound working rule.

For years now we have been delighted to transport ourselves from place to place whenever our choirmaster has accepted an invitation for us to sing. In one huge church with a well-charged, powerful boiler, those of us who stood in the front row had our copies flapping in our faces as great gusts of hot air were repeatedly blown upwards from the grille beneath us. In another, we all began to wheeze asthmatically and feared asphyxiation as soon as we entered the building. The authorities, anticipating a generous response to our concert, had sanctioned the over-liberal use of anti-woodworm treatment, the powerful fumes from which threatened to curtail the whole performance.

Once we were delighted to discover a particularly fine three-manual organ of superb tone which was to accompany us in the exquisite Fauré *Requiem*. As we neared the end of the pre-performance run-through, we became conscious of a curious smell, unanimously put down to contaminated incense. A defective bearing in the organ motor was the true cause, so we had to use the piano instead. I remember various diminutive organs with stops that either came off disconcertingly in the hand or were found not to function when pulled. One celeste produced a loud scrabbling sound, suggestive of hurrying mice, in addition to its own soft tone.

One bitter March day we sang in an ill-heated lofty stone church where our teeth chattered audibly, despite the layered clothing—chic for Antarctica—which we all wore. The wind howled and rumbled ceaselessly throughout the performance and brought tears to our eyes as we left the porch. That place is on my blacklist and so is the other where we were actually promised a 'good meal' which proved to be grey coffee and a few biscuits. We gave brief thanks and rushed for fish and chips, the pub or home as inclination dictated. But we have often found superlative buffet suppers laid out for us.

At St J's, the vicar welcomed us to the vicarage. Cassocked and vigorously inhaling cigarette smoke, he stood just inside the front door, presenting an unconscious imitation of a bored commissionaire as he ceaselessly intoned the repetitive dirge: 'Gentlemen to the right, ladies upstairs and to the left.'

We have sung in aid of decrepit organs, falling steeples, dilapidated roofs, church bells in need of restoration, a parish hall crying out for repair, and woodworm treatment. Numerous charities have benefited as a result of our efforts, including one apparently called 'The Churchunaysher'.

By now, even the shakiest of map readers has reached the parish church of Little Muttering. The choir stalls are inconvenient and a great deal of juggling is required to dispose us in places that are consistent with individual height and the essential part grouping. Crouched and peering, we are now poised for the unseemly leap when we stand to sing. One soprano produces some sinister little black lozenges said to be Caruso's premier choice of pre-performance fodder. We grab greedily and suck expectantly, but —inexplicably—our voices do not suddenly achieve star quality.

The run-through is terrifying in its incompetence. The basses go flat, the sopranos, compensating, go sharp. The altos mumble unintelligibly and the tenors get lost. A strained smile on his face, false confidence all too apparent in his voice, our choirmaster gives us hollow reassurance, saying that he knows everything will go well later on. Our spirits reach their nadir.

But the first anthem goes well and so does the next; we become a little over-confident. My neighbour is hurrying, so, with a disapproving frown I nudge her and she draws rein. Smugly I continue, but pride is my undoing for I come in a beat too soon, only to receive a kindly, unobtrusive elbow in my side. I evaporate shamefacedly with a rash of cold sweat over my face.

There is some light relief later on when our brilliant accompanist, struggling manfully with the eccentricities of an unfamiliar organ, pulls out the wrong stop. For a brief second an extraordinary noise disturbs the air. He catches my eye as he pushes the stop in and winks broadly in his mirror. Forgetting that I lack the safe shelter of an organ loft, I ill-advisedly wink back. Our myopic conductor spots me and, mistaking my *vis-à-vis*, grins conspiratorially back.

The concluding anthem is the glorious six-part anthem *Sing Joyfully*—Byrd, a great favourite of ours, known as 'Sing joyfully, bird!' For all of us, the supreme pleasure and reward lies in working at fine music and learning to sing it to the very best of our ability. The ensuing entertainment is quite incidental.

Please Send   by Alice Mary Merchant

That children change little over the centuries is shown clearly by a bundle of schoolboy letters written more than a hundred and sixty years ago to parents who were ancestors of mine. Such letters vary greatly, from the weekly duty letter to the longer one inspired, perhaps, by a touch of homesickness; but one feature is common to nearly all: 'Please send . . .' Here is one from young John Bewley, placed with his brothers in a Quaker school at Ballitore in the north of Ireland in 1793.

> My Dear Mother,—I now write to thee. I like to be here very well. I am learning Numeration. I send thee my love. I send thee a map of Antient Greece. Yesterday was fine and frosty, and I am learning to slide. Please thee to send me a knife and a top. I am they dutiful son, John Bewley.

And John's brother William writes:

> Dear Father,—I now take the pleasure of writing to thee. Thy cloak is yet here. I send thee four Maps. The Hats which thou mentioned in John's letter are come. I am learning Latin Grammar

and Geography. The Master's hay is mode and we do be making the hay. The boys go into the garden every day to eat fruit. I would be glad that thou wouldst write to me by the man that will bring our clothes. I would be obliged to thee to send me a top, and a tin writing box like the one my uncle sent James. I am they loving son, William Bewley.

Postage in those times was an expensive item, and packages were often delivered by passing friends or servants. 'Dear Father,' writes James, 'I now take up my pen to inform thee that we are all well. The bearer is my friend Samuel Shaw. I was very much disappoint that I did not get a letter by the boy that came for Thomas Goodbody's horse. The Master has got home his hay. Please thee to send my Robinson Crusoe.' George describes a new machine for threshing corn:

Dear Father,—I am now going to relate that walk we took about two miles from this. We went there 5th day last to see a new-fangled machine for threshing corn, it both thrashes and wins the corn. It is turned by two horses, there is one person puts the corn into it and another man to take the straw away. As fast as it is threshed the corn flies off and the straw drops. We were used very kindly by Lady Bountiful, she gave us apples and bread. I am learning Virgil's Æneids Book 1 and Euclid Book 6. We go into the water every fine day. I thank thee for the Magic Lanthorn. Please to get a coat and britches for Benjamin, and please thee to send me Addison's Works, and a black ribbon.

The request for a ribbon followed a death in the family. Unusually precocious is the interest one letter shows in the affairs of their elders. 'I am very glad to hear that my Uncle Thomas is going to get a wife,' James writes to his mother, 'and I hope he shall have success, please let me know if he has. Please send me by George when he returns to school a new penknife and a little stone bottle and a thing for grinding paint on with holes in it. I would be obliged to thee.' In another William writes, 'I am very glad to hear that my Mother has lay in of a young son and I believe his name is Alexander. Please send . . .' That the boys were in no way neglected is shown by this letter:

> A week ago we went to a famous waterfall 10 miles from this by Holywell. We went into a pleasant shrubbery, at the bottom of it was the waterfall, and at the top a shell house, and a little cave cut out of a rock and 2 more that were built, and nicely mossed, and we sat in one of them and after were climbing up the rocks then went to dinner and got Porter and Cider to wash down our round of beef which we brought with us. Please send me a polished wood box to keep my pens like the one Aunt Mary sent to James.

The writing is in best copper-plate style throughout, and some neat maps are enclosed, with an occasional drawing. Seldom does a note of homesickness creep in, but a delicate hint is sometimes conveyed, as in: 'The Mistress has made her currant wine. My father said that he would bring us home when the fruit would be ripe. Please send . . .' The request here was for story-books, gloves, a penknife and more paints. And the eldest brother evidently takes his responsibilities very seriously:

> Dear Mother,—I now write to thee to tell thee we are all well. Benjamin is growing a pretty good boy. James doth desire a coat. Henry hath need of a coat also. Benjamin hath only one pair of britches. I would be obliged to thee to send him one. I would be obliged to thee to write to the Master not to let William be drinking the ink. Would it please thee to send . . .

No, it was not a top nor paints that John wanted, nor a penknife. Brother John was growing up; he wanted a cloak.

Country Wedding
by Joan Kent

My sister's young man spent one glorious autumn afternoon in 1927 oiling and shining four sets of harness for Dad, and cutting enough chaff to fill the mangers for a week. Then, with blistered hands and aching back, he took the plunge and asked Dad for his consent. Only the most persistent suitors reached this point because Dad, though no tyrant, regarded them all as dog foxes prowling round his sheep.

While Mum and Dad were closeted in the dairy and my sisters set the tea-table, my three brothers tormented the perspiring visitor, though the oldest was in no position to tease. He was courting the orphan girl who was employed as lady's maid at the Manor but was in fact an overworked, underfed, underpaid slavey. We called this delicate girl Half-pint. Dad solemnly warned my brother that she was a poor doer, but he could not fail to like the dainty happy girl.

The tea poured out and the meal started, Dad pronounced judgement. He thought my sister could have done better, but accepted the fact that her admirer was no 'Whitechapel bird-catcher'. Mistakenly we children took this to mean a man from London who caught finches and skylarks for sale in the market. As to the date of the wedding, Dad consulted his red diary, presented with the compliments of Cooper's Sheep Dip, and decided on the beginning of December; the black sow would have farrowed ten days earlier, and no other event important enough to postpone a wedding was likely just then. We would all be back to normal in time to kill a pig and pluck poultry for Christmas. He added, to everyone's amazement, that since the cowman's cottage was empty, now that the corn it had housed since threshing time was safely at the chandler's, we might as well have a double wedding and get it over. My brother choked and Half-pint sat completely stunned, for she had not yet received a proposal; but Dad had taken the decision and that was enough.

The best white sheets were mangled twice in readiness for use as tablecloths in the old farm kitchen where the wedding breakfast was to be laid. When the day came, the bus-driver we knew as the Flying Dutchman drew up in the yard with a load of guests, mostly members of our family. Clad in breeches and leggings and an aviator's helmet, he decided to come too, leaving

'Uncle Bill . . . tap-danced and sang'

his few remaining passengers to walk the last two miles of their journey. Aunty Florence, who had recently been 'saved', enlivened the service by calling 'Hallelujah!' and 'Praise the Lord!', throwing the vicar so far off balance that he asked twice if anyone knew a just cause or impediment.

After the feast the men went out to see to the animals, while the women cleared away the remains. The carpet was removed from the large front room, and all the upstairs chairs were added to its existing furniture. The room heaved with people, and one by one each did a party piece. Uncle Bill, a dapper little man who believed that only fools and horses worked for their living, tap-danced and sang 'Oh them golden slippers', accompanying himself with Mum's best apostle tea-spoons. As an encore he did a soft-shoe dance, and we sang 'Lily of Laguna' with him. The

Three men of Wales: John Davies, Thomas Jones, and Lewis Morgan

Morris men of Finchingfield, dancing on the Green in an Essex village with ducks on the pond in the foreground

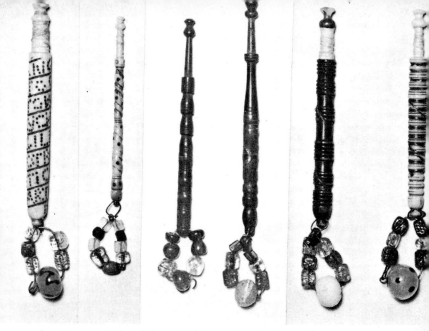

(*above*) Lace bobbins (*left to right*) heavy bone bobbin with rhyme tattooed round the stem, small bone bobbin for carrying fine threads, carved bobbin in wood, carved wood bobbin with band of silk, bone bobbin coloured dark green decorated with brass wire, bone bobbin decorated with brass wire; (*below*) spinning: County Clare, Ireland

(*above*) Aldbury in the Chilterns, Hertfordshire. Georgian and earlier brick and tile buildings around a central pond; (*below*) Latimer in the Chilterns, on the Buckinghamshire-Hertfordshire border, is a Victorian model village which has hardly altered since its inception.

Midland cruck cottages: *(above left)* a Worcestershire cruck house at Wick, nr Pershore, *(above right)* a Warwickshire cruck house at Maxstoke, *(below left)* a Herefordshire cruck house at Putley, *(below right)* a Gloucestershire cruck house at Didbrook, nr Winchcombe—one of the finest in the country

(*above*) Church and Cottages, Cavendish, Suffolk. The Cottages which had fallen into disrepair have recently been skilfully restored, and their interiors modernised; (*below*) The Old Mill, Rossett, Wrexham, built in 1474—rebuilt in 1661

Ruins of crofter's cottage, Glen Torridon, in National Nature Reserve below Ben Eighe, Ross and Cromarty, N Scotland

(*left*) View over Hugh Town, Scilly Isles;

(*right*) thatching at Lustleigh, Devon. The thatcher is completely reroofing this cottage

(*above*) Sheep in churchyard, Spalding, Lincs; grazing by sheep in some villages is a simple solution to the problem of keeping the churchyard tidy; (*below*) Highland school; this study in concentration comes from the little village of Inchnadamph in Sutherlandshire, North of Scotland

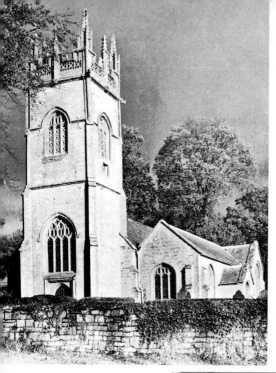

(left) Church at Hatch Beauchamp, Somerset, just before the breaking of a thunderstorm;

(right) a regular customer—a little boy chooses his sweets in the village shop

(right) A woodcarver with a mallet and gouge carving native wood near Barnstaple, Devon;

(left) a laddermaker shapes the rungs or steps for a ladder with a primitive tool, holding the wood in a simple vice

(*left*) A parson stringing up leaves of his home-grown tobacco to cure;

(*right*) a Devon pigman, trying to protect his trousers with a sacking apron from the buckets of swill or wash he carries

(*above*) Sheep washing in Wharfedale; with forked wooden poles the man and boy push the sheep under the running stream to cleanse their fleeces before sheering; (*right*) ploughman's snack; the ploughman eats his bait while his horses feed from their nosebags near Salisbury

(*above*) The Smith's Arms at Godnanstone in Dorset is reputed to be the smallest inn in England; (*right*) the Cat & Fiddle at Hinton Admiral in the New Forest—a picturesque thatched inn very popular with visitors to Hampshire

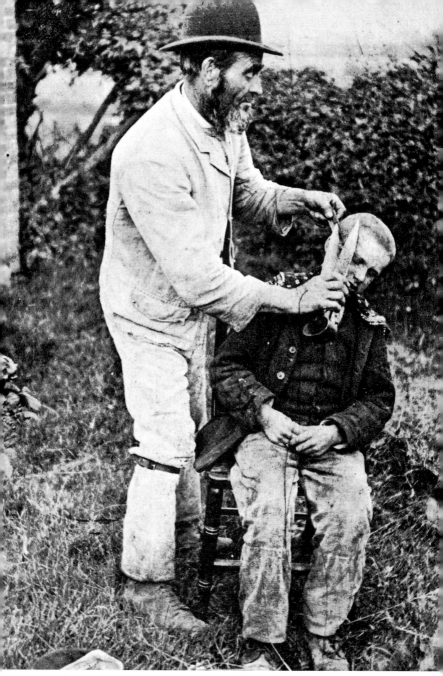

Saturday trim: Jabez Moore, a sheepshearer, trimming an ox-boy's hair with his shears in Kincardineshire, Scotland, 1889

Pictures in farmhouse and cottage: *(above)* hunting scene; *(below)* a winter scene, carrying home the fuel

Flying Dutchman played the mouth-organ, stopping only when his walrus moustache blocked the reeds. Dad, looking straight at Mum and bringing the colour rushing up in her throat, sang a little Cockney song, 'Dear Liza, sweet Liza, if you dies an old maid you'll only have yourself to blame'. My brothers and sisters danced the Charleston, and Aunty Florence prayed that there would be no judgement on them. The horsehair of the sofa pricked the gap between my woolly knickers and long socks, as I

'The bang never came'

sat squeezed between Aunty Betty boiling in her plum velvet and Aunty Florence in black silk, rigidly controlled in the iron-maiden corset that prodded my hips. Release came when Dad said, 'Quiet, please, for little Joan,' and I obliged with 'There are fairies at the bottom of our garden' in my off-key treble.

The song reminded Aunty Betty that a trip to the bottom of the garden was indicated. She took the hurricane lamp left in the porch for that purpose and departed. In the comparative calm that comes when refreshments are being handed round, a high-pitched scream followed by a series of squawks sent everyone rushing to see what was happening. Her velvet dress in complete disarray, tripping over the underclothing she had not stopped to adjust, Aunty Betty fell into Dad's arms, declaring that something had bitten her. She took Mum and the older lady guests to the scullery to show them the proof.

There was much conjecture as to the animal's identity, ideas ranging from a rat to a horse, and my youngest brother slipped out quietly to check that his ferret was safe in its hutch. Dad took the twelve-bore gun from the hooks on the beam and, followed by the men, disappeared round the back of the small building. With my brothers holding a lantern on each side and an uncle ready to fling the trapdoor open, he prepared to fire; but the bang never came, because the noise and light terrified the chicken that sat crouched between bucket and wall. The hilarity and teasing caused Aunty Betty, majestic as a duchess, to retire to Mum's bedroom to regain her composure. It turned out that the hen-house had been shut before any of the chickens were in for the night, and there was much lantern-lit prodding among the fruit trees while the protesting fowls were rounded up.

The Flying Dutchman now declared that it was time to go, and the bus filled up with departing guests, the last aboard being my sister and new brother-in-law who had to sit on the step. As they rattled across the yard we stood around, surveying the chaos, suddenly tired and irritable. Dad took the back-door key off its hook, then hung it up again, because he could not bring himself to lock the door with two of his brood on the other side. Mum came in with the candles, and we waited for our goodnight kiss. 'Thank heaven that's over,' said Dad. 'Two down and seven to go.'

Uncle Charlie   by Joy Charles

My Uncle Charlie was a country parson, enormous in stature and, indeed, in heart, with a flowing mane of white hair. He was charming, kindly and loved by all who knew him. 'But why,' we nephews and nieces asked ourselves, 'did he take an orange and an old teapot to the loo each time?' The fact that he wore a tartan rug slung round his middle like a gigantic kilt, into which were stuffed such delights as an ear-trumpet, a tin of black-currant pastilles, and his latest sermon, was not considered particularly strange, but the orange and teapot?

He suffered badly from arthritis but was always ready to go wherever his parish duties took him, sickbed or pithead, where he more than once remained all night, comforting all who, after an underground explosion, waited for news.

He would pray loud and long in church, for those in need, by name, and especially those in hospital or ill at home. Many is the time we hugged ourselves with delight as Uncle Charlie boomed out, 'Has anyone seen the bit of paper with the sick on it?'

He had two churches in his charge, and took Sunday morning services at both, with only a short break in between. This necessitated a Primus stove and a saucepan of porridge being set up in the vestry of church number one so that he could breakfast before travelling to church number two. A small choirboy was detailed to pump the Primus and stir the porridge at intervals throughout the service, and the resulting noises mingled strangely with the Book of Common Prayer.

His churches were lit by lamps and candles only, and hardly heated at all. I remember one glorious Evensong when the sleeve of his surplice caught fire during a grand gesture too near a naked flame. He ignored the incident completely and beat out the flames with his hand, without pausing in his sermon for an instant.

When he retired he sent me, my sister and some cousins to his study to choose something for ourselves to keep to remember him by. He actually allowed us to invade this holy of holies on our own. The awful thing was, that we none of us wanted anything.

Without the enormous figure in the tartan rug, the room was empty for us.

A Saddler's Bells   by George Ewart Evans

Herbert Bayles was saddler and harness-maker in the Suffolk village of Stradbroke, where he was born in 1861 and died seventy-five years later. Of slight build, with sensitive features, he wore in later years a large drooping moustache which combined with the twinkle in his eye to give him an air of good-humoured benevolence. In addition to running·his own business he was telegraph-messenger and, for forty-seven years of his working life, verger, steeple-keeper and clock-winder, as his father and grandfather had been before him.

Only rarely did his duties clash. Then his friend Harry Webb, the postmaster, was usually involved; telegrams, even when they were tapped out in Morse code on the one line that kept Stradbroke in touch with the world, would wait for no man. The postmaster summoned his messenger by stepping out of his side door and ringing a small handbell to a set formula: *a-ding-a-ding* seven times, with a peremptory coda *A-DING*. At the sound Herbert would drop the harness he was working on, throw his apron over the counter, grab his jacket and hurry to the post office to earn his fee—twopence or more according to distance. On one occasion the brisk *a-ding-a-ding* found him in the tower astride the bell-frame, greasing the bells ready for the Easter services. As he took some time to extricate himself, Harry kept popping in and out of his office, and the furious ringing of his little bell brought the mild comment from wondering neighbours: 'Harry's whoolly riled. Harbut 'on't come!'

Bell-ringing was as important to Herbert as his business. He specialised in the handbells and had a fine collection of fifty-six, the largest of which was an inscribed presentation E flat, as wide across the mouth as a small pail. At the other end of the scale was Herbert's own particular bell, the smallest in his collection. This was often filled with whisky on an outing.

One of the choir boys who was in the handbell team has described how Herbert prepared them for these ringer's outings at the Christmas season. He wrote the tunes out on paper which he pasted on large sheets of cardboard and stood on an easel. The young ringers grouped themselves in a half circle about him. It did not matter that none could read music; each bell was given a number, and these were written plainly in large figures with blue and red pencil. Then the sequences were practised until every boy knew precisely his entrances and exits in the various patterns of sound.

During World War I most of the handbell ringers were, perforce, young boys; and the verger taught them, in addition to the more usual programme, contemporary 'pops' like 'Tipperary', 'Keep the Homefires Burning' and 'Pack Up Your Troubles'. This kept them interested enough to come regularly to practices. Herbert often worked on these tunes in his shop when he should have been finishing a farmer's harness. He would experiment with one, humming it over to himself to get the note, and having identified it, immediately convert it into its appropriate figure. If the farmer came for his harness, Herbert hurriedly thrust the numbered sheet under the counter and picked up awl, needle and thread.

One of his most important jobs at the beginning of this century was to toll the death bell. The tenor was used for this, but first it had to be raised—no easy matter for a small man, since it weighed more than a ton. Herbert often got Fred Amies, the blacksmith's son, to help him. Once the bell was raised, mouth uppermost, and set against the bell-stay, the verger could manage by himself. He placed his watch on the window-sill and kept his eyes steadily on it. Exactly five minutes after the raising he pulled the rope just the required amount, and the bell, being set at handstroke, went through its revolution and came to rest at backstroke, giving one blow of the clapper against the metal. This manoeuvre called for fine judgement and the skill of an experienced ringer; it would have been easy to muff it altogether.

Herbert rang the bell once every five minutes for an hour, following the ritual with utmost care, both to preserve his reputation as a ringer and to ensure that the dead man got full measure of scrupulously observed respect. In the intervals he would record at the side of the ringing-chamber window the date and the age of the deceased. There were scores of entries in black pencil on the limewash; and also one or two special records of tolling with clappers muffled on the deaths of Queen Victoria and Edward VII. Alongside this rather sombre list was a sketch in blue and red pencil of a memorable sunset that had touched the old verger's imagination as he stood at the west window waiting for the minutes to go by. Unfortunately a tidy-minded restorer has since cleaned up the bell-chamber, and this record of part of Herbert's life has proved as evanescent as the sound of his bells.

William Barnes   by Sir Newman Flower

Until a few years ago the poetry of William Barnes, and even his name, were comparatively little known outside his native Dorset, but of recent times, his fame has spread. Much of this wider recognition is due, I think, to repeated talks about him and recitations of his verse which have been given over the radio. Fame waits long for those it wants to crown. But Barnes was crowned by Tennyson, Thomas Hardy, and Edmund Gosse as one of the greatest poets of his time.

The son of a farmer, he was born at Rushay in 1800, and went to the National school at Sturminster Newton. Then he became a clerk in the same small place, which meant being buried under a mass of red tape with small chance of advancement. He educated himself almost entirely, and to such good effect that he took over a school at Mere, in north Dorset, when he was twenty-three. Twelve years later he migrated to Dorchester and became headmaster of his own school, first in Durngate Street, until he bought an old house in South Street and moved the school into it. For the last twenty-four years of his life he was rector at the little village of Winterborne Came, three miles from Dorchester.

During these years he wrote much of his best verse. My father's home was a mile away, and Barnes often used to walk into the house for tea or midday dinner, just as my people went to his rectory. He would come and enjoy the simple meal that was going, and, so one of my aunts told me, had a great liking for treacle tart!

Quite apart from his poetry, Barnes had gifts amounting almost to genius in many directions. He could speak the languages of Europe, with the exception of Russian and the Scandinavian tongues. I have been told by one who knew him that he could learn a European language in two months. He had a vast knowledge of Persian and Hebrew, and could read most oriental languages. He wrote books on the tongues of many nations, and for some of them received no more than £5 each, which was the price of profound knowledge in those days.

All his earlier poems were written in ordinary English. He dropped into writing in the Dorset dialect when he was thirty-three. He said it was the only form in which he could express himself naturally. He wrote his diaries first in German and Italian, and then in Italian till the end of his days. But he preached his sermons in the Dorset dialect because he believed it to be the true Anglo-Saxon root. For one of his first books of Dorset poems Barnes received only £15. At a later stage his publisher told him that if he would write in ordinary English his sales would be much greater, and he reverted to it after a time to some extent, but he was never so happy or so inspired as when he was using the dialect. Consider the calm and beauty he attains in describing a Dorset Sunday:

> In zummer, when the sheädes do creep
>   Below the Zunday steeple, round
> The mossy stwones, that love cut deep
>   Wi neämes that tongues noo mwore do sound,
> The leäne do lose the stalkèn team,
>   An' dry-rimm'd waggon-wheels be still,

An' hills do roll their down-shot stream
   Below the restèn wheel at mill.
O holy day, when tweil do ceäse,
   Sweet day o' rest an' greäce an' peäce.

Or consider, again, this plaint of winter beating on an old wall:

But now when winter's raïn do vall,
An' wind do beät ageän the hall,
The while upon the wat'ry wall
In spots o' grey the moss do grow;
The ruf noo mwore shall overspread
The pillor ov our weary head,
Nor shall the rwose's mossy ball
Behang vor you the house's wall.
Ah! well-a-day! O wall adieu!
The wall is wold, my grief is new.

Barnes was not only a poet but an artist and an engraver. In his early days he engraved his own drawings, and made some beautiful woodcuts of Dorset churches and scenes. Some of his earliest woodcuts were for a printer in the Blackmore Vale, that part of Dorset famous for its butter and cheese. The printer was a poor man, and he paid in cheese and bindings. Barnes was also a fine mathematician. One of his close friends of these early years was General Shrapnel, the inventor of the shell, whom he helped with many of the mathematical calculations, apostle of peace though he was. In short, anything that interested Barnes he quickly mastered. He was deeply immersed in science; he lectured in the subject and wrote a book *Exercises in Practical Science*. He did not regard as adequate the geographies served out to school-boys in those days, so he wrote his own, and his *Outline of Geography* was a far more efficient book for pupils than any then sold in the shops. Incidentally, his daughter who wrote his life said that he always allowed the character of every pupil to shape itself, and that he never beat a boy except for lying. In his later years he acquired some good pictures with his small means. I have a Wilson oil painting of his, 'The Three Marys', a Resurrection scene. On the back of it is inscribed in Thomas Hardy's writing, 'Bought at the sale of William Barnes's effects by T. Hardy'. To me it is an invaluable treasure, having been owned in turn by two literary masters of my county.

As the years drew upon him, Barnes gave up his school and contented himself with his labours in his little Dorset parish of Winterborne Came, his readings from his works in various towns and villages, his friendships, and the considerable correspondence that flowed in upon him from admirers of his great culture, and from those as learned as he. The snows of years began to whiten his long hair and beard, but he could still be seen walking about Dorchester, dressed like a Quaker of romance with close-fitting breeches and stockings and buckled shoes, his long coat and wide Quaker hat. Passers-by saw the old man creeping along the pavement like a figure from yesterday, his blue eyes bright with greeting to anyone he knew, his back bent a little now through the passage of so many winters and summers.

At eighty-six, his intellect and his memory were as keen and alive as ever. An aunt of mine—in later years I well remember her striding slowly up and down the dining-room of my father's home, a lean, gaunt figure, reciting poem after poem by Barnes in the most beautiful Dorset dialect—went across the fields to see the old man in his last days. He was lying in bed dressed in scarlet robes like a cardinal; his long white beard flowing over the sheet, so white that it was difficult, at first sight, to differentiate the beard from the sheet. And on his face was that smile that had always lived there. Only a few days before his death he dictated to his daughter—not wrote—what is considered to be his finest poem in the dialect of our county, 'The Geäte A-vallen To'. The last verse expresses so truly the memory he left behind him:

And oft do come a saddened hour
   When there must goo away,
One well-beloved to our heart's core
   Vor long, perhaps vor aye.
And oh! it is a touchèn thing
   The lovèn heart must rue
To hear behind his last farewell
   The geäte a-vallen to.

For some days after his death the gate was propped open so that it should not be 'a-vallen to'.

The day on which William Barnes was buried had been one of cloud, but as Thomas Hardy was walking up the lane towards Came, a sudden burst of sun threw its gleam upon the hearse. Hardy found in this his last remembrance of William Barnes and, in this sweep of light, he bade farewell to him. When he returned to Max Gate that evening he wrote to his memory the poem, 'The Last Signal', which ends:

To take his last journey forth—he who in his prime
Trudged so many a time from the gate athwart the land!
Thus a farewell to me he signalled on his grave-way,
As with a wave of the hand.

These final lines reveal all the depth of affection which Hardy felt for his friend.

6 Where the Cottager Works

Proper Ole Wagg'ner   by F. F. Nicholls

Of all the farm work I have done the long hot summer spent with
Prince in 1947 was the most pleasant. He was an elderly shire
gelding, and we were employed ambling on odd jobs around the
lanes and undulating fields of a sprawling farm on the North
Downs' edge. The soil was thin and studded with huge flints,
and the fields were sheltered by shaws—thick belts of woodland.
It was a lovely stretch of Kent, where you valued a horse's company, for you would work all day without seeing a soul.

My rise from waggoner's mate to under-waggoner was absurdly
rapid by nineteenth-century standards. I began as mate to
Arthur that spring, working with his horse Nobby, another shire
gelding, half Prince's age and full of strength and devilment.
Our first job was drilling mangolds with an old steerage drill
which set two rows at a time. I had to lead Nobby for, as Arthur
said, he was 'same as all you young chaps, too silly to goo steady-
like'. So I spent dusty hours holding him back with an aching
right arm, dividing my attention between keeping the wheel in
the last track and my fingers out of the continual working and
champing of those great yellow teeth. 'Ah,' said Arthur apologeti-
cally, ' 'e's a good 'orse to pull, but 'e can be a nasty ole sod wi'
some people. Give 'im 'alf a charnst, 'e'll ver-soon 'ave yer.'

When the first two tiny leaves of the seedlings were visible
against the soil Arthur took his oil-can and spanner over to the
three-furrow horse-hoe and set the tines as close in to the plants
as he dared. Then started another spell of slow mechanical
pacing. Up and down the rows we went, the spring days passing

in a pleasant tedium. Several times my mind wandered, but Arthur, though seventy, was much more alert and would suddenly break in: 'Whoa—beck, Nobby! Gawd, Oi don' know if you ain' a tidy chap, Fred. Jiggered if you ain' missed a row again. You keep all on thinkin' about that gel a yourn, that's what 'tis.'

I was even less successful on the one occasion when we changed round. We were hoeing three rows at once with that tool, and the sense of responsibility was too much for me. Just let one tine hit a big flint, and the whole tool-bar jumped a few inches to one side; before I could do anything several feet were cut out of three rows of tender seedlings. 'Let me have Nobby again, Arthur,' I begged, when this had happened a few times. 'Ah, you ver-soon lorst yer nerve, then?' he said with a grin and went back to the hard work on the handles like the gentleman he was.

When I look back on my short career as a waggoner I realise that most of my early troubles arose from this tactful courtesy of the experienced hands. Any local boy of twelve could have done the jobs of which I was making such heavy weather, so they were reluctant to offer any comment, other than a bit of leg-pulling, on even the most ludicrous mistakes. If there was comment it was most apologetic: 'You don' mind me tellin' you, but you gorn an' tied that waggin-rope to one a the spokes, Fred. You start up loike that, Oi don' know what-all you won' break.' But generally they were too polite to tell me, and I was too ignorant to know there was a difficulty until disaster struck. Even when, in turning a fourwheeled waggon too tight, I snapped off a gatepost with the back wheel Orrie, the farm foreman, only tilted his cap back, scratched his head and grinned: 'Well, Oi don' know if you ain't a tidy bleedin' 'erbo! Still, nemmine, eh, Fred? That ole post was rotten as a pear, any'ow.'

The hoeing done for the present, a day came when a small banky field was to be set with kale. To my delight and pride Arthur found another mate to lead Nobby and told me to 'put ole Prince inter thaddair roller an' goo on ahead of us. We'll give yer time to git a coupla wents done 'fore we start drillin'.' (A went is a waggoner's term, going back to the fourteenth century at least, for a complete journey with an implement from one side of the field to the other and back. Half a went is an een.)

Prince took one look at the roller, another at the steep slopes of the field and another at me, and decided on the tempo of work for the day. 'Ck-ck! Giddup!' and he started in a rather hurt and reproachful way for the shaw at the far side. There he tore off a spray of sweet-chestnut leaves, nodding idiotically as he waved it about and pretended to enjoy chewing it. That removed, he shuffled grudgingly round, turning the roller, and seemed suddenly to remember that the gate to the road now lay ahead; once he got there he might be taken back to the stable. So without a 'giddup' or a 'ck!' he threw his shoulders into the tugs, making the harness creak and jingle, and stamped off buoyantly up hill and down, his great feathered feet biting into the dry soil. Of course a bitter disappointment awaited him at the gate, where I began to turn him round, and his second sortie to the far hedge was even more infirm and aggrieved than the first.

A competent waggoner would here have asserted his authority by tuning up old Prince's backside a bit, but I did not know what pace to set for that horse and that roller, and I was too weak (or humane, if you prefer it) to make him go faster. Consequently I had not got much done when Arthur and John arrived with Nobby and the drill, and I soon became aware with something like panic that they were catching me up. Arthur had noticed it too and commented severely: 'Come on now, moi Fred. You 'adder make 'aste more'n this. That ain' on'y a light roller, y' know. Make 'im work, let's git on, git out of it.'

As I worked across the field, another difficulty caused more delay; I could not keep that roller going straight. Since then I have seen textbook photographs of horse-rolling where the waggoner, walking right behind the roller, ruled beautiful die-straight lines across a flat fen field. It was not a bit like that with me: I had not got those long reins, and Prince would never have moved if I had been that far away. So I led him, and dog-legs soon began to appear in my rows, posing the dilemma: should I leave that dreadful sight to Arthur's gaze or try, by setting the roller right in, in places, to get my lines straight again? To this day I never mow my lawn without facing the same problem.

Soon Arthur and John were so tight up behind me that I was turning at the headland under their critical eyes as they waited for a chance to do their next went. 'Course,' said Arthur, 'days gone by they wouldn' a let you turn a roller loike that. See where you got that ridge a soil up on the inside? The olé bailee wouldn' 'alf a given you a shirruckin' for that.'

In the middle of the afternoon we finished rolling and drilling. I took Prince out of the roller, to his immense satisfaction, and Arthur prepared to take Nobby away; but poor Prince had not finished his day yet. From the cart Arthur produced his trace harness and a set of light harrows and proceeded to give me a rare and very brief bit of instruction: 'Put ole Prince's trace 'arness on an' put 'im in them 'arrers. If 'e gits 'is feet caught up in them chains, kick 'im in the guts.' Then he left me to it. I was quite sure I was not going to follow his advice, whatever Prince got caught up in; he told me later that Prince's one drawback was that he had been hurt in the back legs by a smith when he was young and could not abide anything rubbing up against them. The harrowing was less of a strain to both of us than the rolling, as no one was breathing down my neck now; but the lines were, if possible, even more crooked.

Young Arthur, the waggoner's son, and John, the other tractor driver, had just put their machines away and were standing outside the shed as Prince and I came through the quiet yard at knocking-off time. Both grinned broadly, and Arthur turned his face, which was that of a ruddy, good-natured, gabbling raven, to his mate: ' 'Ere 'e comes then. Beggared if 'e don' look loike a proper ole wagg'ner; on'y wants a whip an' a pair a yorks.'

I used to enjoy everything to do with stable-time—the jealously guarded quarter-hours during which (in theory) we tended our horses. I liked the stable atmosphere, a century-old blend of the smells of hay, cake, old leather, horse's sweat and urine, and shag tobacco; the knock of a curry-comb against a stall; the music of our spacked [hobnailed] boots and of the huge polished shoes of the horses on the knobbly flint floor; hearing the contented muffled sniffing as they demolished the hay and oats in their mangers, while Arthur and I talked, perched on corn-bins. After fifty years as a waggoner Arthur could sit on anything, however hard, sharp or narrow, and still look comfortable.

That summer now seems to me a procession of golden days of sunshine in which old Prince and I kept 'sojerin' on', doing all manner of odd jobs. Every morning after breakfast and the work conference in the yard, Prince would back gingerly from his stall and swing his front shoulders round to follow me out of the half-door. Often we would be doing jobs on our own: a load of sheep-gates to the field of kale, some straw for a steddle, a water-barrel for the sheep in thirsty weather, posts and wire, loads of coal and water for the threshing tackle—we were a rural tramp ship. So hours and miles passed, the sun hot on the back of my shirt as I led the old horse about or, when my waggon was empty, sat on the front, watching the stately elderly stalk of his back legs. 'Course,' said Arthur one day, as I rode into the yard, 'one time a day, there, they wouldn' a let you roide about loike that, nemmine whether you was empty or not. You 'adder walk; you'd git some ear-'ole elst.'

Then there were other spells of regular hard graft: when we went dung-carting, for instance, in the old style with two carts, two horses and three men. And I remember a week of burning June sunshine when, with the help of a steam-roller which made even poor old Prince dance in his shafts, we made up the road. Down to the wood we went where, in a glade quivering with the still heat, lay great piles of flints, all picked by hand from the ploughed fields in years gone by. We loaded the flints with heavy stone-spuds, the sweat stinging in our eyes; then back into the full blaze of the sun, Prince's hide plastered and glistening with sweat.

We toiled away to the chattering of the mowers, and soon came the crown of the waggoner's year, the idyll of the hay-rake and swath-turner—light pleasant jobs, sitting comfortably on proper seats while others heaved with forks under a settling pall of dust and seeds to pitch hay on to the elevator or stack it as it dropped off. At first I sweated and pitched with them, my face and neck wetly coated with dusty itching seeds, envying Arthur as he drove the side-delivery rake up and down, forming four swaths of hay into one windrow. But when about half of the first field had been swept up by the tractors, I was able to stick my fork thankfully into the ground and walk back to the cool dark of the stable, where Prince was munching quietly. I put him into the rake and drove back along the narrow lane, to the apoplectic annoyance of a whole column of motorists who were trying to get to the coast and were dissatisfied with Prince's 3mph. If I had had the moral courage I would have turned round and addressed them as did the waggoner in my grandfather's favourite story: 'Whass the matter with you lot, then? Oi are gooin' as fast as you are.'

Once in the field, starting what was to me a new job, my early troubles returned. That fatal tact of my work-mates plagued me again, assisted this time by a certain self-confidence. The idea, I knew, was to rake up and down the field, releasing the rake at the same points each time, so that the rakings formed straight rows. That alone took a bit of practice; but my real mistake was to begin by drawing the rake along the crooked hedge bordering the road. As my course was not straight, my lines of rakings, though straight, were not parallel; and as I worked out from the hedge, two rows would converge until only a few yards apart, so that there was barely time to let the tines down in between them; two others were so far apart that Prince was hardly able to shift the rake, so full did it become of hay.

Eventually Arthur happened to notice this increasingly farcical situation and came across. 'Whoi, whatever are you doin', mate?' he asked, more in incredulous amusement than in anger. 'Oi don' know if you ain' made a proper beggar-up a this. Ole Stuart won' 'alf give you some ear-'ole when 'e sees this turn-out. What you 'adder do, see, is make what they call a strick-out—goo straight acrawst the field. You wanner fix yer eye on sup'm, say a tree in that ole shaw, an' goo d'reckly for it. Then keep the rest a yer rows straight with that, an' yer rakin's 'll be straight. You mu'n scratch about loike an old 'en, y' know.'

As the last of the wide dry acres passed under the tines of my rake the binder made its first round in the winter oats, spitting the first untidy green and yellow sheaves into the hedge-bottoms. Back went Prince to the green peace of the paddock, while all of us trudged round after the binder, shocking the oats, then the barley, then the wheat. Scarcely a drop of rain fell on the ripening ears, and it was not long before the old horse went back into the shafts of the light trolley to begin the last of his many harvests. Arthur and Nobby took the heavier, but much more beautiful, Kent waggon, built like a boat with hardly a straight line, with posts called stifers fixed in rings at each corner to support the load.

Surely of all the manual jobs man undertakes the harvesting of a field of corn by horse and waggon must be the best to do and to look back on? With the glorious weather of that summer, work soon settled into a routine: after breakfast Arthur and I rattled about the yard with the dung-carts, doing odd jobs. Once the dew was off the shocks we drove out to the fields, taking a pitcher and two loaders, who would stay out there all day; the easy pace, the squeak of the wheels, the gritty tingle of the iron rims on the flinty road, the leisurely talk and chaff of men dangling their legs over the sides of my trolley: it was hard work and yet a holiday too.

The pitcher and I would get down opposite the first shock. Prince's reins would be coiled over the near-side hame of his collar. The sheaves would be casually tossed on to the floor of the trolley, and as casually kicked or twitched into a neat row down each side, 'arses out'ards'. I would walk to Prince's head, calling out 'Stan' 'ard!' as a warning to the loaders, and without another

THE COUNTRYMAN COTTAGE LIFE BOOK

word Prince would throw his weight into the tugs and move off. Stop and start, pitch and load, till the loaders were dark heads against the sky, men in a world of their own; then, 'Fill in yer middle.' A few shocks later, over with the waggon-ropes, and the loaders would come swinging and slithering down the front of the load, put one foot on Prince's backside, another on the shaft, and so jump to the ground.

Then they would walk off to load the waggon, leaving me and the old horse to get our swaying, bouncing load back to the yard. When we got there I backed him close into the stack with those hind feet of his gingerly shuffling and his lean hams thrust into the breechings. I had to be tactful to get him to do it at all, for he hated backing; so one hand would be gently on his nose while I murmured encouragingly Arthur's formula, 'Git beck, me ole cock-burrd.'

It was a few days after harvest that the farmer and I stood in the stable, talking about Prince. 'That ole horse don't owe me anything,' he said. 'He's been a good ole tool. Funny thing, the day I bought him in Ashford market a little ole half-diddecoy sort of chap came over and said to me quiet-like, "Ain' no call fer you to say nothin', but that 'orse you jis' bought won' pull." Fancy that, and ole Prince has been one of the best I've ever had. Poor ole feller, he's just about past it now though; I'm afraid he'll have to go before the winter. I'll see him shot here though. I wouldn't like to think of him hauling his innards out in Belgium for another coupla years.'

I left the farm in September, and I heard later that old Prince had indeed gone. Since then most horses of his kind have followed him to the knackers, bringing to an end an era and a skilled craft, and taking with them one of the great interests of farm life (ask any small farmer over forty). And yet on the whole I think I am glad their era is over. The surface romance of the horse was a façade behind which there was much overwork and ill-treatment. Arthur was a kindly man who loved horses, yet several times I saw him carry out on Nobby the measures he recommended for

Prince; and he told me that the standard treatment for any sign of vice in a horse was to 'tie 'im up an' beat 'im till 'e croid loike a babby'. Working heavy loads over unmade tracks and wet fields is bound to involve tremendous effort for the horse and times of infuriating frustration for the carter. I hated to see the desperate heaving and floundering of a beaten horse; but if he is so minded, a man can kick his tractor to pieces for all I care.

Blacksmith's Striker   by W. B. Harvey

The kitchen was silent except for the ticking of the wall-clock and the occasional dropping of cinders in the grate. The blacksmith slowly finished lacing up his boots, bending down from his chair at the table where he had just finished drinking tea, so that I could not see his face. Having tucked in the last end, he straightened his back, sucked the drops of tea from his drooping blond moustache and regarded me solemnly.

'Bill,' he said reproachfully, 'you know the business wouldn't stand it.' I felt like some Brutus who had stabbed a dying Caesar in the back, instead of a sixteen-year-old blacksmith's striker *cum* house-boy *cum* post-boy who had asked for a rise.

'All right, Mr Oxley,' I said with a lump in my throat, 'let's forget about it.' But I knew it probably meant the end of my job with him; I would have to look for a better-paid one. My fourteen shillings a week were barely enough to keep me, and my father's little farmstead was not doing too well. It would be the end of a life I loved, but there was no future in it for me.

It was just after six o'clock in the morning, and we were about to sort the mail for the village of Kingston, near Canterbury, where he was blacksmith and sub-postmaster. At six-thirty we would start on our deliveries, he on the big round of about nine miles and I on one about two miles shorter. He would go through the village to the rectory, Kaysers, Court Farm and along to Horse Head, Dunkin, Little Dunkin and Covet Wood farms. My round lay up over the hill above the Dover road to all the farms, farm cottages and houses between Poorstart and Ileden.

When the mail was sorted I started off on my bicycle, a bit sad at first; but youthful resilience and the lovely morning in late spring soon made me forget my troubles. By the time I arrived at the clump of red pines standing out starkly against the hill-top skyline at Ileden, I was singing at the top of my voice. A casual kiss from the housemaid at Ileden House, and my cure was complete. I rode along the crest towards Poorstart, full of cheerfulness and hope. I would cut teasels and sell them in Canterbury market, I thought, or snare rabbits and sell them. There were heaps of ways of making money to add to my fourteen bob. I would even eat less, though this was not a happy thought as I felt the first pangs of a huge appetite for breakfast.

I free-wheeled down the white chalk road towards the village, calling a cheerful greeting to the road-mender who was breaking a heap of flints half-way down. Hallo, I thought, old Jim at work already. It must be after half past seven, and I have the forge fire to light, my breakfast to cook and eat, and one or two odd jobs to do before the blacksmith comes into the forge at half past nine.

I pulled up with a jerk at the forge door, threw the old bone-shaker aside and went in. There was the familiar scene—a long low workshop cobbled at the end where the horses were shod, earth-floored at the other end where stood the great hearth with its big concertina bellows. Rows of horseshoes hung from racks overhead; bars of grey and rusted iron rested on the rafters. The water-tank at the end of the hearth was festooned with hammers, tongs, punches, swages and all the other tools of the blacksmith's trade. By the side of the hearth stood the anvil. In a corner was a drilling machine, antique-looking even in those days, forty-odd years ago.

I soon had the forge fire blazing merrily and, with a few strokes on the handle of the bellows, brought the coals to a red glow. I put on my can of water for boiling an egg, and another for making tea, and by eight o'clock I was sitting at the bench eating and drinking with a will, all thoughts of curbing my appetite forgotten. After breakfast I cleaned up the forge, banked the fire and went out to groom the pony and tether him on a wire in the field to graze. He was a playful little beast and often nipped me when he got the chance, but we got on all right and were never happier than when he was jogging along in the shafts of the trap, taking me and a load of parcels to and from Canterbury each Saturday.

When the pony was gone, I mucked out the stable, cut some chaff, chopped firewood and cleaned the tricycle which was the

'There was the familiar scene'

pride of the blacksmith's wife. Then it was time to get back to the forge, and before long old Oxley came in, still looking a bit stern and quieter than usual. But soon we were in our usual pleasant frame of mind with each other; he was not one to bear a grudge. We had a shoeing job in the afternoon, but in the forenoon we were to fit a set of tyres for the wheelwright. There they were, new and resplendent, two big wheels and two smaller ones for a haycart. The size of the iron tyre was found by 'running the wheel' with an iron disc. This looked simple but was highly skilled; you could wobble the disc and get quite the wrong measurement.

When we knew the sizes of the tyres we got down strips of iron and cut off the right lengths, allowing for the weld. We warmed each strip in the fire and hammered it into a circle, first cutting and tapering forks in the ends for the weld. The forked ends were then raised to melting point and, at the moment when the metal ran, we whipped the strip out and on to the anvil. The white-hot iron shot out a shower of sparks under the smith's blows as the weld was made; and the colour faded gradually from white to yellow, yellow to orange and orange to dull red and blue-grey as he shaped and finished it. While he put the final touches to the tyre, I rolled the wheel across the road to the wheel-pit, where I laid it down the huge hub resting in a central depression and the rim on the brick circle.

The bellows wheezed and clanked as I brought the fire to a roaring heat, and the smith shifted the tyre round in it until the iron was red-hot throughout its length. Then, 'Right, Bill,' and, seizing the glowing circle with tongs, one on each side, we rushed across the road and lowered it into position round the wheel helping it down with one or two blows from a sledge. Clouds of steam rose as we shrank and hardened the tyre with buckets of water. Lastly nails were driven through holes into the felloes, and the job was done.

One more big tyre, two smaller ones and the forenoon's work was over. We were both smoke-blackened and sweating, and I was ready for dinner. Away I went on the old grid-iron, three miles down a narrow lane, to rabbit stew and dumplings which tasted better than anything I have tasted since, as did the rice pudding and jam which followed.

Back at the forge I got down the set of shoes for Jack, one of the plough horses from Poorstart Farm. We had sets ready made for all the horses in the neighbourhood, and as soon as Jack was shod, we would make another for him. Jim Quested, the horseman at Poorstart, had secured Jack in the shoeing bay and now joined the knot of onlookers in the smithy doorway. The big shire pawed the cobbles restlessly and eyed the smith warily as he approached.

'Get over there,' roared the smith, giving Jack a crack in the ribs with his hammer. 'He-e-e-ah,' replied the horse indignantly, aiming a kick at the smith in return. When this customary exchange was completed, they settled down to business. With a tap of his hammer on the offside foreleg, the smith raised the hoof on to his knee. In a few minutes the old shoe was off, and the hoof was being trimmed for the new one. This was tried on, given a

'Clouds of steam rose as we shrank and hardened the tyre'

few shaping blows at the anvil and laid in the fire to warm up for burning on. With a spike thrust through one of the holes the hot shoe was fitted on the hoof, burning itself into a comfortable fit. The smell of burning horn that accompanied this operation is still in my memory, and the smoke-wreathed scene of man and horse is clear in my mind's eye.

The blacksmith nailed on all four shoes and turned the job over to me for clinching up the nails and giving the hoofs a coat of stockholm tar. I was not yet trusted with the nailing on for difficult or big horses, though I had shod ponies complete and had nailed sets on one or two other horses. It was a tricky operation, and there were many snags. The horse would lay over on you, if it thought it could get away with it, using you as the fourth leg instead of standing on three. Many a time the smith, seeing me sweating under a horse' had walked over and cracked it in the ribs with a 'lay over there' to make it stand up. Now I could keep it over myself. If the nails were driven in awkwardly they could touch the frog, the sensitive part of the hoof, and the horse would go lame. I remember the first time I went to work on a hind hoof, I was about to place it between my legs, as was done with the fore hoofs, when the smith gave a great shout and his hammer came flying in my direction.

'Get out from under there,' he shouted. 'That horse'll have you up on that rafter as soon as look at you. You don't sit on her hind hoof.' And I was shown how to put the hoof on my lap from one side.

When the shoeing was finished, and the hoofs had been raised on to an iron tripod in turn for polishing, Jim Quested took the horse away and we got on with making the new set. I enjoyed this. The smith stood by the hearth side, one hand working the bellows while the other handled the tongs holding the iron in the fire. He might have been some old Norse hero, with yellow hair and moustache, tawny down on chest and forearm, and leather apron moulded to his form by many years of wear. The haze of smoke, illumined by the slanting rays of the afternoon sun and the glow of the fire, lent a kind of mystery to the scene. At a sign from the smith I picked up my sledge and stood ready. Out of the fire and on to the anvil came the iron, and the rapid cling, clang, thud of our hammers began, the smith's indicating where I was to strike or, with a double blow on the anvil, telling me to pause while he did some shaping with the smaller hammer. Sparks flew in all directions, and to the group of onlookers at the door we must have looked like two figures in a scene as old as Vulcan.

It was fascinating work. The bar gradually took shape under

our blows, with many rapid changes of position, now round the horn of the anvil, now on the flat. Punches, chisels and swages, each on its long cane handle, were seized from the rack and used to form the shoe, butt up its ends and punch nail-holes, until finally it was finished and thrown on to the hearth end to cool.

When we had finished, the sun was low and the dusk was gathering in the corners of the forge. It was time to go home.

'Good night, Bill,' said the blacksmith.

'Good night, Mr Oxley,' I replied. Our early morning difference was forgotten. Tomorrow, fitting tines to harrows in the fields, we would be back on the old footing. There were better things than money.

George's Raincoat   by Dinah Hamblin

For the first time in four and a half years there was no sign of George. I bumped over the stones in the farmyard at exactly 5.25 am, expecting to see him sitting on a shaft of the old Berkshire waggon. Granted it was dark in the cart-shed. For one thing the rain was teeming down, and it was also the first Monday of summer time, so we were back to starting work in the dark again. As I leant my bicycle against the wall of the shed, I was quite expecting to hear the usual greeting, 'Come on, young Dinah, time we called they cows in.'

As I switched on the yard light, the Guv'nor came out of the farmhouse and Arthur, the cowman, began to call the cows.

'Morning, Dinah,' said the Guv'nor.

'Morning, Mr Bell,' I said. 'George's late.'

'What?' roared the Guv'nor. 'No George? Never been late once these thirty years. Must be ill, that's what. When we've finished milking you'd better go up to his cottage and see what's the matter. Arthur,' he shouted to the cowman, as the cows began to come in from the meadow, 'looks like we're short-handed this morning. George isn't here.'

'Yeh—an' I can tell you why,' said Arthur. 'I'll bet the old varmint never put his clock on.'

The three of us set to work. Soon the familiar sounds of milking emanated from the cowshed and dairy. The teeming rain had slackened, when unhurried footsteps were heard approaching the dairy. George, a tall spare figure in the middle fifties, stood in the doorway. The shaggy eyebrows shaded a pair of piercing eyes. George took life seriously, and his grim expression rarely changed. In the four and a half years I had known him, I doubt if I had heard him laugh four and a half times.

' 'Ad to shelter,' he explained shortly. He never used two words if one would do.

'Shelter?' exploded the Guv'nor.

'Under the firs, on the common.'

' 'Fraid the rain 'll melt him,' grinned Arthur; 'like a lump of sugar he is.'

'Mac lets water,' volunteered George.

'Well, if that's all,' said the Guv'nor, 'you'd better go into town on the bus this afternoon and buy one. Go in on the one o'clock bus and you'll be back by three for milking.'

'Can't,' said George.

'Why not?'

'Ain't got enough money on me.'

'I can lend you some,' said the Guv'nor as he started to walk away.

'Yer,' called George. 'Shan't 'ave time to 'ave me dinner.'

'Why ever not?'

'Gotta walk down to the shop to buy a pie. Shan't 'ave time to walk back to the bus stop.'

'The missus will give you some dinner, so that's settled. Now get a move on, or we shall be keeping the lorry waiting.'

The morning flew by as usual. On reaching the farm with five minutes to spare after the dinner-hour, I met George sauntering across to the farmhouse.

'Missus won't 'ave to wash 'e,' he said, holding up what looked like a clean plate. 'I put'n under the tap in the dairy and rubbed 'n round with a bit o' paper.'

'Aren't you going into town after all?' I asked.

'Ain't time now.'

I was puzzled. 'Whatever have you been doing, then?'

'Eatin' me dinner.'

'What? For a whole hour?'

'Lot to eat,' he explained. 'Meat was tough. There was dump-lin's an' taters, an' a lot o' they 'urricane beans, what I couldn't get on me fork.'

'Well, you've missed the bus now,' I told him.

'Go tomorrow,' he said slyly, with a near grin. 'Did you get that bottle of orange drink at the shop for I?'

'Yes; I'll put it in the dairy.'

Mr Bell wasn't exactly pleased with George's excuses. 'Don't bully him,' advised Mrs Bell; 'he has a "thing" about going into town. Says he's sure to get knocked down by a bus or steam-roller. He'll go tomorrow.'

We all thought so too, when he turned up next morning in clean dungarees and jacket. But, as we finished our various jobs at midday, he announced 'Shan't go to town today.'

'Why ever not?' questioned the Guv'nor.

' 'As to keep runnin',' replied George.

'Running?'

'Yeh—was up an' down all night. All young Dinah's fault.'

'My fault?' I exclaimed.

'That drink you bought for I. Was all right till I drank that.'

'What drink was that, Dinah?' asked Mr Bell. 'Orange squash? That shouldn't have upset you, George. How much did you drink?'

'All on't.'

'Perhaps you didn't put enough water with it,' I suggested.

'Water? I never put no water. Drank it out t'bottle.'

Definitely it would be unwise for George to venture into town that day. And the next two were out. One was early closing in our small market town, and on the following day the men were busy sowing and George could not be spared. On the Friday morning the Guv'nor told him he might as well go and do his bit of shopping that afternoon. But, when I got back to work at one-o'clock, the first person I saw was George.

'No one o'clock bus today,' said he smugly.

'Why not?'

'Time's altered. Goes at quarter to.'

'Did you know that this morning?' I demanded in as severe a tone as I could manage.

'Ah, ole Dan Penny was sayin' summat about it in the Wheat-sheaf last night, but I wasn't rightly listenin',' admitted George.

'What shall we do about him, Dinah?' said Mrs Bell later in the afternoon. 'I can't help feeling sorry for him, living alone as he does, and scared of the unfamiliar.'

'What about getting a catalogue and sending for a coat?'

Mrs Bell though that was a good plan: she had a catalogue handy and we soon found what we thought would suit George, so the idea was put to him. He tried to be *blasé* about the whole business. Eventually he chose the colour and style. I wrote the order and enclosed a cheque. In less than a week he was fitted out with a good hard-wearing macintosh. 'Just the job,' said the Guv'nor. 'That should keep you dry, George.'

Two mornings later the rain teemed down as I bumped over the stones in the farmyard at exactly 5.25 am. There was no sign of George. ' 'Ad to shelter,' he explained, when he arrived twenty minutes late.

'Shelter!'

'Under the firs, on the common.'

'Where's your mac, man? Where's your mac?' roared the Guv'nor.

'What, my new raincoat?' said George. 'I ain't goin' to make 'e wet.'

7 The Post Office, the Flower Show and the Pub

Room at the Inn   **by William Gooding**

'There's six boats coming in from the moors,' I said to Father on a winter's evening. From our inn I could gaze across the floodwaters of Tealham Moor where the small lights, bobbing like fireflies, were zigzagging nearer. Half a dozen customers in flat boats lit by hurricane lanterns were coming to spend the evening.

Overhead the painted sign of grouse and pheasant creaked on its hinges, and the light of the door lanterns reflected the gold in the tail feathers of the cock. Near by, for dry-land customers, there were mounting steps and a great iron half-hoop for tethering horses. The boatmen would drive iron spikes and chains into the grass bank at the bottom of the hill to anchor their craft.

'Put the iron pokers in the fire, Willie.' Father, who was serving home-made cider at fourpence a pint, knew all his customers. 'And get out the canister of ginger. They'll want it mulled tonight. And put a fresh loaf on the bar. Maybe they'll want toast in it.'

The pokers would be red-hot, the two-handled pints of cider ready laced with ginger, by the time the chilled boatmen came. Into the cider would go the flaming poker, making it hiss and rear up in a spiral of white froth and fragrance, and the broken toast would follow into the steaming brew.

'Ah, 'tis a good drink,' said George, our oldest customer; ' 'twould drive the chill out o' a corpse.'

The whitewashed Somerset inn was at the top of the hill. On warm summer days the cider mugs stood outside on the broad shelf of the half-door. The long low walls were covered with pink roses in season and decorated by the pronged spears of the eel-fishers, the tall black hedge-nets of the starling-catchers and the decoy traps of the goldfinch-cagers. An immense orchard lay to the side. The walled garden was lined with greengages, Victorias and loganberries, and from the bar window customers might see water being winched from the well in an old oak bucket.

The inn was also a general store, a place of sale and barter, and in the wet season an unofficial *poste restante* for letters which could not be delivered over the floods. Letters were rare but always hoped for: 'Biss thee got a letter for I this marnin'?' If so, it would be stuck between two cider jugs on the shelf. Father would hand it over and, often enough, give a hand with the reading.

The bar with its old beam, fireplace and two oak settles

The shop, an old stone-flagged store next to the bar, was filled with the odour of corn and candles, tea, spice and bacon. A row of iron-hard scarlet Edam cheeses stood on an upper shelf. If a customer was so pinched as to want but half, Father would cleave it with an axe kept for the purpose.

'Han't thee got no Zalmon's tea?'

This was highly prized by boatmen and landlubbers alike, being the first product ever to give coupons for prizes. There was no substitute. 'Us'll wait. Missus'll drink watter firrst.'

The shopping was sometimes packed in a basket, but more often into a scarlet kerchief big as a bedspread. This was first removed from neck or knees, spread on the counter as groceries were pell-melled in, then knotted at the corners round a stick which took it to the waiting boat.

In the bar, with its huge fireplace and two oak settles at one end, the old beam was clustered with brilliantly shined horse-brasses. Copper bowls filled with marigolds and nasturtiums stood in the windows, and sometimes an old blue jug with Cheddar pinks. There was an ancient hurdy-gurdy and a shove-ha'penny board: these and muzzle-loading took up most of the evenings. Brass powder horns came from huge gaming-pockets, and the rammers rhythmically packed home the powder, while smoke rose to the ceiling and conversation on seasons, markets and harvests burred on.

The spiral stair went round the chimney-piece. Every evening I took my scrubbed night-face and my candlestick through the bar on my way to bed and was greeted by a chorus of: 'Good-night, Willie my zonner! Sleep well!'

My bed was above the bar. Lamplight filtered through gaps in the rafters; mingled fragrance of mulled cider and tobacco caressed my nostrils. The clang of mugs, the tinkle of the hurdy-gurdy, tumbling ha'pennies, the talk in rich rolling Somerset usually sent me off to sleep soundly; but occasionally I would put an eye to the widest crack in the boards. Below might be a wild duck or teal waiting for a swop, or pale green duck-eggs in a basket of rushes, cheek by jowl with a dead rabbit or hare. Pigeon, snipe and partridge found their way in, and once only I spotted a bunch of larks, legs tied together. Father, shocked, turned the gypsy away with, 'Us likes our larks to sing round here.'

Bartering went on endlessly. Out of the boats came gigantic white celery streaked with black peat soil, dinner-plate-sized mushrooms, clutches of peewit's eggs and black floury potatoes:

On the way to bed

'Who'll buy my chiddies! Six shillin' a hunderd.' He would be a while selling them. These were the 'twenties when money was scarce.

Auctions were a different matter. 'Who'll bid me for this fine hayrick?' called for carefully counted cash or the rarer cheque book. They took place in the afternoons and were improved by a pint of cider or, occasionally, a beer. Beer was a poor second, and we sold no spirits. Cider was king.

Sunday mornings in our inn saw a two-handled quart mug being filled with cider and passed from man to man, each taking a quaff. The mugs always bore the entwined wheatsheaf and plough device and the old verse, often jovially recited aloud:

> Let the wealthy and great
> Roll in splendour and state;
> I envy them not, I declare it.
> I rear my own lamb,
> My own chickens and ham;
> I shear my own fleece and I wear it.
> I have lawns, I have bowers,
> I have fruit, I have flowers,
> The lark is my morning alarmer.
> So, jolly boys, now
> Here's God speed the plough,
> Long life and success to the farmer.

The cider-making house behind the bar was large, dark and impregnated with the smell of fermenting apples. Hogsheads stood in rows, some unbunged and topped with wooden funnels, others runnelled as though by a white creeping lava which poured in ferment down their sides to the floor. The press, filled with pommace, was in the middle. Every couple of days, as the pommace squeezed out, Father would cut round it with a hay-knife and clap it back on top under the screw. When it was dry, the wheat-straw was taken carefully away to be used again and the dry pulp was shovelled into farm carts. Cows loved it mixed with bran.

All day, in our green-apple harvests, tall empty baskets

beckoned in the orchard. They ended my mole-catching revenues. I liked to sit with penknife and barrel-stave making a snare, threading the six holes with copper wire and a long switch of pliable ground ash, then setting it with muddied hands in a field on the way to school. But this and the joys of fishing, and of riding cart-horses out to distant pastures for pennies, faded away before those apple baskets.

'Willie,' was the cry, 'what are you wasting time on? Get into the orchard.'

When it was not apples it was hogsheads. They needed cleaning for the new cider. Last year's sludge was poured out to nourish the apple trees. Drunken ducks flapped and cavorted riotously round me while I scrubbed and swilled out barrels with fresh spring water.

Morgan Sweets, the earliest apples, made the thinnest and least popular cider. Later, mixed crops of Warner King, Tom Putt, Horslyn and Ribstone Black made a fuller better-flavoured drink. Father's cider was a simple matter of apple juice and brown sugar, but our bar held gilders of lilies: 'I be puttin' a raw leg o'

lamb in each o' my hogsheads thissen year,' or 'I be puttin' a bottle o' brandy in a special hogshead every year till me boy be twenty-one.' But, good or bad, it all went down.

Before the Show   by Margaret Macbrair

There is no close season for flower-show meetings in our village. It takes almost four months to clear up the accounts after one show; then it is time to begin preparations for the next. There is usually one particularly tangled meeting in mid winter when both events are on the agenda. But with only a month or so to go to the day, we are all clear which year we have in mind, though we may still be hazy about the date. This is because the show is held on the Saturday nearest to the feast of the saint to whom the parish church is dedicated; indeed it is believed to be a secular carry-on from the medieval patronal festival. Doubtless the system worked admirably before the Reformation, but in these apostate days not every one has the saintly calendar at his finger tips and only the belated publication of the schedules

finally settles the matter. Immediately a good section of the committee reveal that they have arranged their holidays at that very time; newcomers to the village are hastily co-opted and the paper strength of the membership rises from thirty to forty.

All the same, this time-honoured method of fixing the date brings a feeling of inevitability to the last, most vital, most confused of the annual cycle of committee meetings. To begin with, it is held on a different day of the week and in a different place from all the others, so that about half the members are late or do not turn up at all. Last year it landed in the village hall and I arrived half an hour late, having been assured by a neighbour that I had got the wrong evening. So I sat well at the back but in a good strategic position, next door but one to the Chairman's wife. Often there are so many little chats going on that one can get at the Chair only by putting a question to this lady, who then relays it in tones he cannot fail to pick up after fifty years. Unfortunately at the moment she was fast asleep.

But above the peaceful murmur of private conversations and from the Delphic haze of his pipe smoke the Chairman recognised me. He leaned on the rickety card-table, removed his pipe and addressed me: 'Ah, we were just discussing the ankle competition you ran last year.'

I raised my eyebrows, as I could remember almost nothing about this attraction. 'Perhaps it was my husband . . . ?' Several ladies giggled; I floundered on: 'I think the doctor judged it last year and he's going to be away this time.'

My neighbours on one side were planning an expedition to buy prizes for the hoop-la; on the other they were arguing whether the cookery expert from 'The Gas', who judges the curiously named Industrial Section, did or did not have lunch with the men who judge the vegetables and flowers. A member in the front row soon put a stop to this; although reputedly deaf, she turned round to say loudly, 'She's not coming this year anyway.'

The Chairman gave another oracular puff at his pipe and said nothing; the Secretary, on his right, glanced at a few papers, then at us, but also remained silent. In the eighty years of its recorded history the show has had only three secretaries, and nobody now remembers when the present one took office. The Treasurer, seated on the other side of the Chairman, leaned across to whisper something. The Big Three nodded.

I hoped the ankle competition might be swept aside, but as a silence even longer than usual now ensued I started desperately to fling questions about. 'Well, what time is it to be held? Last year it was nearly forgotten. Will there be an entrance fee? Who's going to give the prize?'

'It's difficult enough to get them to enter; they'll never pay,' the Chairman's wife suddenly threw at me, then dropped off to sleep again.

'Well, thank you very much,' said the Chairman, taking his cue, 'you'll run it again.' A pause while he shouldered the burden of speech once more: 'Now about the tent stewards . . .'

'But we can't fix the time of the ankle competition until we

know when the prizes are being given': I clung to the shreds of organisation.

'Five-thirty': it was the Secretary's turn.

'Then we'll have it at five.' No one contradicted me, so I relaxed and looked round for someone to chat with; it was essential to collect some local news for my family to make up for their small and hasty supper. The Chairman's wife had opened her eyes again, so I made good with a fire of questions about the health and achievements of village children. All around me members muttered, 'They'll be away,' or 'They won't be here,' as the previous year's list of stewards was read out. 'Well, there's the vicar,' put in a chapel-goer. 'He'll do it,' promptly replied the Anglicans.

So we left the stewards and went on to the rota of sitters at the gate who take the admission money. As by now everyone present had at least one job, we all suggested absentees. No names were rejected; I think but am not sure, that the Secretary made some notes. At least an hour had passed.

'Well, if that's all, thank you very much, ladies and gentlemen . . .'

'What about the teas?' came from the front.

'Well, I did ask Mrs Harris again.'

'Did she agree?'

'Er, not exactly . . .'

'Did she refuse?'

'No, but . . .' Around me breaths were drawn in and glances exchanged. Now we were really getting down to it; this was the key position, and the show only two weeks away. 'Tell you what,' another puff at the pipe, 'shall I call on her tonight?' We were all appeased.

Voices rose again: 'The tents are costing more than ever this year.' A friend leaned forward to get on with arranging about an adaptor for the projector at the next Women's Institute meeting.

'Well, I couldn't help steward, 'cos of my leg, see?' An elderly member turned round to tell us at length how he had received a mysterious blow on the knee.

'I think I really must go': the lender of the garden for the show, and therefore the most important person in the room, rattled her matches hopefully and lit another cigarette.

'Well, ladies and gentlemen, if that's all . . .' came again from the haze of smoke. But the meeting was getting its second wind. 'What about the . . . ?'—and on it went. Subjects were brought up again and again, nothing was settled, round and round we talked, and the air grew thicker. Yet no one really worried; it was as though we were simply fulfilling a ritual. Somehow, partaking of the nature of the huge vegetables and magnificent flowers that appear annually, are judged and disappear, the show seems to have an organic life of its own. We knew that it would take place and be the customary success, whether or not a single coherent decision were taken in the village hall that night.

The Post   by Wendy Wood

Rab, the regular postman of Glenbog, was taking his late autumn holiday, so the job had to be done by someone else in the glen. Tommy Beag leaned across the counter of the tiny post office and thereby revealed the reason for his nickname Small. 'Well, Andrew, I could do the post round, yes,' he agreed. 'But I could wish it were summer, for myself and the pony will not be any earlier from the railway station than Rab was, and that will be five o'clock and it dark. I hope there'll not be too many parcels. I don't like them parcels. Long ones like corsets for Bella, and ones marked "Glass" all over for the Big House.'

It was indeed no small undertaking: the railhead was eight miles away along a bridle-track, and on return the pony was left in the post office field and the letters delivered on foot. For a week Tommy enjoyed the cups of tea at the many crofts, and the importance of being the bearer from the outside world of news which lost nothing of drama in its inaccuracy. On the Thursday he had left a good supper simmering in the iron pot beside the peat fire in his cottage, a combined poaching effort having resulted in a generous distribution of venison; but that night he did not return to eat it. He lived alone, so he was not missed till the morning, when somebody heard his cow calling out to be milked and organised a search party.

'It was all the fault of that damned calf of Schokie's,' Tommy complained later. 'I left the bag under a bush at the Gorstan because it was heavier than the few letters left in it; and when I got back, hadn't that hell of a stirk streeled it right across the Auchmor? So I was late and thought I'd take the short cut. It saves nearly a mile that way, up and over the hill, but it's not my side of the glen. I was all right up between the two Big Rocks and down the Lag [hollow] and along the Shelf, and to the Big Flat. Dhia! It was the blackest night ever I saw; but I was all right with the bright torch—that's what I thought. More fool me. For just when I was at the top of Sgurr na Moine [the peat bog] the light got terrible weak. I had two new batteries in, so I thought it might be the spring needed something more of padding. I took a bit paper out of my pocket and sat down on a rock and opened up the torch.

'Man, it was quiet—quiet and black. Up there, backwards to the west and under the shoulder of the hill, there wasn't even the difference of blackness that the sea usually gives. Like being inside a small box it was. The sheep was all low down—no birds. It was worse than the look of the end of the world; you'd think it had never begun. I had the two ends of the torch in my hand. I pushed the spring up—nothing but a wee glim like a *cuileag-shniomhain* [glow-worm]. So I knew it was the bulb that was not screwed down tight, and I undid the top. The silly wee footling pip of a thing! Didn't it fall out of my fingers? I said to me, "Tommy, this is when you don't get flustered", and sat where I was, bending down to feel with my fingers; grass, heather, wee stones, I could feel them all, but no bulb. Then I went on my knees, searching all around, and I prayed, indeed I prayed, for the thought of going back beside the precipice or on by the bog bridge put such fear on me that I was shaking like a *critheann* [aspen].

'But what was the use of sitting there? I could feel the cold eating into my bones. A match? Amadan! Do you think I would not have made a torch of the heather if I'd had a match at me? I was near the panic that tears the head off you; but I knew it was thirteen hours before a glim of daylight, so I just had to go on. You know the bog bridge, the raised curved bit, only twice the width of a foot? If there had just been a star or two; but there was a drizzle of cloud and no sky. Daft-like I shouted, and my voice melted just in front of my face. I felt as if I was the only person left in the world.

'Well, I went forward, just putting a foot at a time and it not leaving the ground, and at last I knew I was on the turf bridge. I tried not to think of the black oozy clabar below me on either side that would suck me in and close my eyes and stop my mouth. I was on all fours now, putting out my hands this side and that at the edge of safety, and then, being fairly sure of myself, I stretched down on the left—solid ground; down on the right—nothing. And I couldn't stop. I was away to bloody hell. My body tipped. I grabbed at nothing. I let out a scream. It's a wonder you didn't hear me ten miles away. Then the God of Mercy hit me on the head and I was nowhere.'

'Well,' said Andrew, 'if you had always brought the empty bag back to the post office you would have been sooner missed. Them silly torches. If the thing goes out, then you're worse than you never had it. Damn it all, man, when we found you, there you were with a small hole in your head, below the edge of a 12ft drop and nowhere near the bog, or the bridge that is in it, and the good doctor says it'll be a while before you're on the post again. Maybe Rab will be back from his holiday by then.'

'If I am for it again indeed it will be three torches, and a bit candle and matches I'll be taking,' said Tommy, 'and I'll be keeping to the proper path.'

What? No scampi!   by H. F. Ellis

They say that the old country pub is diminishing alarmingly in numbers. The brewers, intent on modernising and 'rationalising', scrap three and rebuild one, so that any small loss in convenience and cosiness for their old customers is amply compensated, in their view, by a handsome neo-Georgian façade behind which green plastic chairs, set round circular glass-topped tables, form an ideal setting for the consumption of hygienically-wrapped meat pies.

There are other agents for change besides the brewers (some of whom, to be fair, have a proper appreciation of pub life and carry out any necessary rehabilitation with discretion and understanding). There is the now almost insatiable demand of the British people for food. Bread, cheese and pickled onions you used to be able to get, with luck, in a small country pub; and perhaps, in the more advanced establishments, a packet of biscuits from a glass jar. Even this modest lunch was an event a little out of the ordinary, watched with a kind of slow astonishment by the regulars as though a man with such gross appetites had not come their way for years. It is a bit different now.

Any pub with less than six varieties of sandwich to offer is clearly scheduled for demolition. Women demand coffee. 'What? No scampi!' cry scandalised motorists, deceived by a bold 'Snacks at the Bar' outside. The regulars themselves, who in the old days would no more have thought of going to a pub to eat—unless it were something they had brought along themselves in a handkerchief for half-past-tenses after four or five hours in the fields—than they would have thought of going to church to play whist, are not altogether proof against this wholesale gluttony and often munch crisps in a deafening way.

This is only the lower echelon of pub eating. What of the ancient inn, with nothing about its modest exterior, except perhaps a couple of Jaguars and an Aston Martin, to show that so much as a cheese sandwich is obtainable within, but which produces, almost as soon as one has set foot in the bar, an undoubted waiter bearing an 18in by 12in menu at which the Emperor Vitellius himself might have flinched? It would scarcely do to ask for a pint and a pickled onion here. The rich country dialect of Tom and Dick, that used to rumble and reverberate about the blackened beams, is no longer audible; instead, Chris is asking Tony and Fiona whether they want their Camparis straight or Americano. In the corner of the settle, where Harry brooded for hours over a mug of cider, Mr Egon Ronay himself (or is it half of Bon Viveur?) is sipping chilled sherry and wondering whether to delete 'Quick, friendly service' from the next edition and substitute 'Getting altogether too big for their boots'.

There used to be more laughter in the skittle alley, and you could take your coat off if you wanted to. But that was before it was converted into a dining-room, and certainly it looks prettier now with all those pink lampshades and the racks of claret suspended so quaintly halfway up the far wall.

It would be altogether too deeply dyed-in-the-wool to wish all these improvements at the bottom of the sea. Few people, in their role as motorists, really regret that they can now count on getting a decent ham sandwich for lunch instead of the sad soup and unwanted roast lamb that used to await them at some market town hotel. It is pleasant, too, to be able to dine delectably once in a while, and preferably at somebody else's expense, at a little out-of-the-way inn in the country. There may even be a case, though none occurs to me at the moment, for plastic chairs and neo-Georgian façades.

All I would urge is some moderation, a touch of restraint here and there, in the great leap forward. Let there remain at least one genuine pub within any given area—and I would define that area, if pressed, as one within which a reasonable man might expect to find such a thing. As to defining a genuine pub, that should be totally unnecessary for any right-thinking person who regards the village pub as an invaluable, indeed an indispensable part of country life.

However, for the guidance of those brewers who genuinely want to preserve the real thing, and whose only fault perhaps is that they have never been inside one, I here set down a few principles or pointers. These are mostly negative. There is no definable model, no Platonic 'idea' of the perfect pub stored up in heaven at which all earthly pubs should aim—and if there were, it would be better abolished. Variety and, within limits, individuality are to be prized, uniformity to be deplored. So that it is advisable, in the main to indicate only what a real pub is not.

It is not a 'lounge'. It is not a restaurant. If food is provided—and by all means let that be the case when I happen to want it—it should be unobtrusive, at the back, preferably prepared off-stage. Huge hams, lobsters, great piles of potato salad arrayed along the bar counter itself are an offence in any circumstances, and particularly so to those who cannot afford to eat them. Boiled eggs floating in a sort of vinegar are traditional, as rarely disturbed as the collecting box in the far corner, and may be shown.

There must be no smell of frying. This is as insidious and as inexcusable as piped music. The combination of the two, had Dr Johnson ever experienced it, would very soon have caused him to qualify his famous dictum.

Six horse brasses are enough. Witticisms in poker-work had better be kept to a minimum, too. All that is really required in the way of reading matter on the walls is an out-of-date point-to-point announcement or, for the customer with time on his hands, a sale notice listing innumerable farm implements in nicely varied print sizes and starring 16in-calf Friesians. Inns of historic interest can reasonably display a framed article about themselves cut from a 1912 issue of *Country Life*.

If the landlord is a retired major he should not try too hard to look like one. Likewise, commanders (RN) ought to go easy on brass-bound nautical wheels, sea-urchins and other marine debris. In general, it is wise to remember that the wholesale suspension of articles from the ceiling is a part of the mystery of ironmongering, not inn-keeping.

Any kind of fruit machine is as incongruous as a waiter in a black tie dashing repeatedly across the space between the dartboard and the throwing line.

These are about all the requirements, or non-requirements, of the proper country pub that occur to me. I am tempted to include a directive to the publican to add, below his 'No Coaches' sign, a modest '—and no Jaguars or Aston Martins either.' But what if he has one himself?

8 Pictures and Purges

Pictures in Farmhouse and Cottage   by M. K. Ashby

It is the fashion now to think it the function of a picture to stir
only a pure aesthetic interest. Maybe for this reason, many of us
being scarcely capable of an interest so specialised, we have had
that dullest of fashions, walls bare of ornament. I know several
farmhouses whose recent mistresses have treated all their pictures
as rubbish or lumber. What treasures did they throw away?

On the walls of some farmhouse sitting-rooms and cottages
one finds a charming mixture of pictorial relics. In the course of
years I have made a mental collection of these: it would be a pity
literally to amass them into an assembly of curios. It is their site,
hanging still where they belong, that accounts for much of their
charm. Very varied and often small, they remind one gently and
indirectly of customs and social movements, and of phases of
sensibility in the minds of rural folk. For example, when cock-
fighting came to be frowned on in the early 1800s, most of the
neat, highly coloured little prints of favourite birds were naturally
ousted from their frames in favour of less wicked subjects; but
a few have lingered in dark corners on the stairs or near the bread-
oven in farmhouses I have known. On the other hand, in evangelical or largely nonconformist villages you may see prints of
biblical subjects which pious pedlars brought as late as the 1880s:
Abraham carrying faggots of wood with an innocent wondering
Isaac behind him, or Moses surveying the land from a rocky peak.

It must have been pedlars of an earlier time who carried the
vivid picture-maps of the narrow way to heaven and the broad
road hellwards that I saw in a cottage in the early 1900s. I remem-

ber only vaguely the hard path upwards because, like any good nineties child, I had an adequate sense of sin and turned to study the way on which my feet might be already set. That way shone broad, with many inns, market places and fairs; but I was in a strange cottage, with a load of shyness as well as sin, and left the map only half seen. Perhaps, I thought when I first pondered on cottage pictures, I shall yet see and study the chart of the narrow way. Since that time I have been shown a picture entitled 'The Broad and Narrow Way', of German origin, issued in England in 1883. This, with its pointer to 'death and damnation' and textual references, is eloquent indeed as well as vivid. But a child's memory is very faithful and my mental photograph is of a pair of charts hung one on each side of some large tradesman's almanac.

In cottages, how interesting it is to close a door and find behind it—not considered decorative today—an old certificate of membership of a branch of the 'Foresters' (Greenwood Tree by name, or Ancient Elm) or, dated 1873 or 1874, a warrant of membership of Joseph Arch's Union of Agricultural Labourers. In the fine spacious farmhouse of a Methodist, till lately Wesleyan, family that had once given John Wesley a bed, there hung prints of the founder preaching in Georgia and portraits of other early worthies of his and their church.

Of lighter, perhaps greater, charm are pictures intended only to please. In both farmhouse and cottage one can still see paintings on glass with their odd richness, slight transparency and sombre subjects, and also flower paintings on velvet, dating from the early nineteenth century, faded into delicate beauty. If one of these has been dragged from a dark cupboard into the light of an antique-shop window, the original colours may be excessively sharp, though often the drawing was good. In those that have been long on a well-lit wall the background of velvet, once ivory-coloured, has gained a brownish, almost golden richness, and the colours of roses and cornflowers have undergone odd changes, and all have been brought into harmony by the quieting effects of time; but, because of the clean drawing, a passion-flower or moss-rose spray breaks in lively fashion out of the dim wreath. It is less often that one sees eighteenth-century products: vicissitudes have been too numerous, and dealers too knowing at sales. But I have a little print entitled 'Plenty', one of a set of four representing the seasons, which must have been intended for small country rooms. Set behind an oval of painted glass in a small brass frame is the little pinkish cornfield, and in front of it a classical figure, tall but buxom and stout enough to support suitably a horn of plenty.

When I was a girl, high schools were all the rage, and how we looked down on the old boarding schools to which farmers' daughters had formerly been sent! But certain farmhouse pictures have shaken my faith. There are, for example, the Italian scenes rendered in woollen cross-stitch—often not quite finished, as if after coming home the girls who began them in their last school year never had leisure again. Much rarer are the black-and-white silk pictures, of which I have seen only one or two. From a distance they resemble prints of landscapes; only very close at hand do you discern that they are embroidered with fine black silk thread on a white silk ground. A later fashion, I feel sure, were the wooden or metal panels on which girls painted sprays of wild roses or gillyflowers, and of course the small water-colours. How much greater is the appeal of these modest decorations from the hand of some person like ourselves than that of printed copies of masterpieces! But the high schools covered their walls with photogravures of the Doge of Venice and his like, and made the girls do drawing exercises to pass a series of 'art' examinations.

Of great charm, often, is the occasional family portrait which a farming household treasures—only one perhaps, and that not an oil-painting but a water-colour or a grey crayon drawing with a little bright posy in water-colour and a dash of gold to give youth to the hair; or if the drawing is of a man it may be wholly in crayon, black and blue, or black and brown. These, one hears, were the work of travelling artists, usually done, so far as I can tell, between 1800 and 1840. One should add, perhaps, that the travelling artist is not quite unknown today: in some Cotswold farmhouses are hung recent pencil sketches of the village church or the farmhouse itself. But in general the field has been left to those most hideous of all objects hung on walls, enlarged photographs. They have to be greeted with respect for they so often commemorate missing heroes, but aesthetically they deserve the phrase 'all-time low'. Here is scope for a visiting artist to make small presentable pencil sketches from them and frame them pleasingly.

Returning to cottages, from rather later times we have a type of picture I find very touching. The superior Victorian maidservant, confined except for a fortnight in the year to other people's kitchens and nurseries, had her aspirations. It was she who brought to her mother's cottage those prints of ladies sitting in long trailing white gowns on garden seats reading lovers' letters, or being helped over stiles by gentlemen in clothes of an equally unearthly elegance and brilliance. She also decked the home walls with pictures of a velvet-clad girl kneeling, face uplifted, with an open book in her hand at the foot of a cross washed by wild waves.

How did the labourer before 1914 find pence to frame his beloved certificate, and his wife or mother her Bible pictures? Partly in the same way as he clothed himself, by using other people's cast-offs: sometimes the pictures are in gilt frames, good but ill-fitting. But on occasion he made his own simple four-cross frame, decorated like the old waggons with rhythmic notchings and slicings of the wood. The farm daughters also learnt to make macramé-string frames—just how, I have forgotten; it is so long since I saw one.

Spring Turn-out   by Bridget Wastie

Round about this time of year Mrs Smith has what she calls her 'spring turn-out'. Every second year or so her daughter Mary and son-in-law Ernie arrive from a neighbouring village well equipped to take full and active part in this onslaught. Mary is a fiend for housework. Ernie is maintenance man on a large estate. With them are the two small grandsons, kept all day in a state of miraculous, pristine, unboylike cleanliness by the meticulous Mary who, besides her self-imposed chores, combs, scrubs and washes them with unabated energy. At length the last lick of bright paint has been applied, the last flowery strip of dado stuck on. As Mrs Smith bustles off down the hill to the station with Mary, Ernie and the boys one can almost feel ancient little Pear Tree Cottage relaxing its beams and breathing gratefully, 'That's that.'

About a week later Mrs Smith's voice, rather aggrieved, floats over the loose stone wall: 'You ahn't bin round to see 'ow I be fixed this time.' My own voice, deprecatory and apologetic, replies: 'I know, it's dreadful how time gets on top of one. Shall I come now?' This is all part of the rite that has grown up over the years. If I were to go without being asked I would be given short shrift, I know.

I enter the low-beamed room and give the approved gasp of astonishment mixed with admiration. Mrs Smith is not descended from the original Romany of Wychwood for nothing. The Stafford china (cut to a minimum over the years by the zealous Mary) and polished brass flash and twinkle from their positions on the mahogany sideboard and the shelf over the fireplace. The muted pastels of the geometrically patterned wallpaper surrounded by its flowery dado blend into the shining cream paintwork and startling black of the beams. I take stock of the general effect. 'Why, the sofa's gone.'

'I know, our Mary says there aren't no call for 'em nowadays. Fifty year I'd 'ad that sofa an' 'e wus second-'and when 'e wus bought. There wus two chayers to match 'im, y' know.'

I do know. I saw the two stout mahogany-framed buttoned leather chairs go down the hill two years ago, borne over the heads of the lucky purchasers. If they are sensible, they will still have those 'chayers' when the flimsy modern fireside contraptions which superseded them in Pear Tree Cottage are dust.

'Yes, Ernie 'ad the old sofa out on the garden an' burnt 'im. Three days it took. 'E were a good 'orsehair sofa, y' know.' There is regret in her voice. I know that too. I watched Mrs Smith each of those three days come out into the garden and survey the smouldering ruin like Nero who, for all his fiddling, must have felt a similar pang when Rome burned.

We gaze appreciatively round the shining room. A bright fire burns in the grate. The old oak table is back in the centre of the room covered with a rich red chenille cloth on which reposes a pile of large framed pictures. Mrs Smith picks up a leather and gives a polish to the glass of the topmost one. 'Our Mary says as pictures aren't fashionable any more; but I dunno, I'd be lost without mine; they be old friends so to speak, livin' alone as I do.' This is another regular rite. I always feel like a favoured guest on private viewers' day at the Academy, except that every picture has by now become an old friend of mine too.

Mrs Smith lifts the big enlargement turning slightly greeny-yellow behind the glass. 'Look at 'er, dear old soul—my 'usband's mother; 'er were laundry-maid at a big 'ouse yerabouts. 'Er were a strong Salvationist too. The master at the 'ouse drunk like a fish. It wus a complaint; 'e wus called nebriate—couldn't stop 'isself, y' know. The mistress says to 'er, "Mrs Smith," she says, "you must never fetch the master strong drink, no matter 'ow 'e asks yer." Well one day 'e says, "Mrs Smith, slip across the road an' get me 'alf a dozen bottles o' beer." 'Er spoke up sharp: "Beggin' yer pardon, sir, I be a Salvationist an' I dun't taste, touch nor 'andle an' I can't do it." "Such imperdence!" 'e says. "Take a week's notice. No, you can go now." "That I can do, sir," she says, an' wipin' 'er 'ands on 'er apron she walks out thro' the door singin', "We will fight for the Lord everywhere." By dinner time 'im come up to ower 'ouse. "You be a better woman than I be man, Mrs Smith," 'e says. "Come back an' I'll raise yer wages sixpence." Ten times 'im 'ad 'er on that lark. 'Er started at seven-an'-six a wik. 'Er wus earnin' twelve-an'-six when 'er left, an' that wus money in they days—more than some men.'

Rather proudly Mrs Smith places the indomitable Salvationist in her accustomed corner by the stairs door where, in a chair in the garden among the flowers of a long-past summer, her stiff upright pose and direct glance tell a modern world that she had the courage of her convictions.

The leather skims delicately, gently almost, over the next enlargement of an identical school depicting a young dark-eyed girl in old-fashioned maid's uniform, a streamered cap surmounting her piled-up hair. 'My sister,' says Mrs Smith. 'After the first world war the villages round about wus struck with the 'flu 'demic. 'Er an' 'er 'usband an' little gel was struck down wi' it. I went over to the next village to look after 'em. I shall never forget it. Poor Albert knew 'is end 'ad come. "Oh Lizzie," 'e says, "what'll Louie an' Peg do when I be gone?" "Dun't you worry about they Albert," I sez, "they'll be took care on." I didn't tell 'im they wus both layin' dead in the next room. That wus a sad time fur me. I buried seven relatives in one week.' She hangs a smiling dark-eyed Louie over the sideboard: 'Ah well, they've missed a world o' trouble.' Mrs Smith braces herself. 'I'll put the kettle on.'

While the kettle sings she busies herself with teacups. She puts the tray, laid with an exquisitely laundered tray-cloth, the bright cups and saucers and a plate of biscuits on the table, pushing the remaining pictures to one side. The fire crackles and the smell of the gilliflowers mingles with the aroma of freshly-made tea and home-baked biscuits.

Mrs Smith sips ruminatively. 'I always leaves it a week 'fore bringin' 'em down from the attic where our Mary stacks 'em every time. I think 'er understands underneath though.' She lays a spotless work-worn hand across the glass of the topmost of the three pictures remaining. 'I dun't need to tell y' about 'e; you've 'eard it too often. 'E's never far from my mind. When you gets seventy-odd an' lives on yer own you 'as time to think.' All the same I look with renewed interest at the head-and-shoulders enlargement of a young man in his prime dressed in the uniform of a driver in World War I.

'Ah, I always remembers that big 'ospital in London where I wus called to see 'im. 'Im 'ad bin gassed by they Germans. "Mrs Smith," says this clever doctor, "it's only fair to tell you your 'usband is a dyin' man; 'is lungs be 'teriatin' an' 'e'll get worse. I'm arrangin' fur 'im to go in 'ospital near your 'ome where you can visit 'im till the end." "Oh," I says, "an' what's wrong wi' 'is own 'ome? If 'e got to die, 'e can die where 'is wife an' children can be with 'im." Another doctor spoke up and said, "She be right, it can't do no 'arm; 'e ahn't got more than a couple o' months".' Mrs Smith's voice becomes triumphant. ' 'Im lived ten years, an' I worked my fingers to the bone for 'im an' I'd do it all over again. Night an' day I tended 'im, an' 'e went one June evenin' like a puff o' smoke; I turned to the window a minute an' when I turned back 'im 'ad gone.'

She rises and puts the picture in the place of honour near the fireplace facing her own armchair. 'Ah, they can't tell me about 'ard times,' she says. 'When 'e went I wus left with eight children, a sow an' ten little pigs an' not a penny in the world. But I managed; I 'ad these.' She spreads her bony hands. 'Come on now, another cup o' tea. They biscuits ahn't turned out as well as they might 'a' done.'

She pours the tea and picks up the two small pictures that remain, placing them one on each side of her husband's portrait. 'This be a regimental badge worked in silk when 'e wus ill, and these be 'is medals—an' 'e earned 'em if anybody did.' We drink our second cup of tea and Mrs Smith surveys the room. 'Looks more like 'ome now,' she observes. I agree and after praising tea, biscuits, decorations and hospitality take my leave.

The walls of my own living-room appear singularly devoid of character this afternoon. But as always this will pass, and in any case where among my own relatives, living or dead, could I find one who for sheer dramatic interest could vie with those now once more cosily surrounding Mrs Smith?

Snake in the Glass   by Joan Kent

My brother warned me of the snake inside our lamp. At night it was clearly visible coiled up in the translucent bowl and, when the lamp was filled, I could see it squirming like the viper we once found behind the water-butt.

The lamp had a base of twining iron vines and a multi-coloured globe that radiated light like sunshine through stained glass. It transformed our workaday farmhouse kitchen and was the axis of my childhood's winter world. I treated it with healthy respect, knowing that the snake waited like some evil genie in a bottle, ready to escape and eat whoever broke the lamp. The memory of that Saturday night when it was smashed is with me still.

My mother believed that, if her children started each Sunday clean inside and out, nothing would ail them for the rest of the week. Each Saturday after tea the galvanised tin bath was placed on the flagstoned scullery floor between the copper and the pump; and no matter how warm the water, one had the sensation of sitting on a cold wet slab. Being the youngest, I came first in the assembly line, but all six of us eventually progressed to sit in cotton nightshirts, drying our hair in front of the kitchen fire.

Medicines for both humans and animals were lumped together on the same high shelf and, after baths were over, Mum lifted down a square yellow tin. This, according to its deceptive label, contained a brand of wonder lozenge that cured coughs, croup and consumption. Gathering us round her like a hen with worms for her chicks, Mum stood over us, ladling out great lumps of green gritty liquorice powder into cups of senna tea. We would have preferred the worms. To our young minds Saturday night without liquorice was the main attraction in marriage.

Anyone with a skin blemish was treated to a dose of brimstone in black treacle as a Saturday evening second course. The horses were sometimes given the same mixture and, as Mum used to say, 'Show me a horse with pimples.' Chilblains and sprains were vigorously treated with rubbing oil; the label on the bottle showing both horse and groom proved conclusively to Mum that it was intended for man and beast. Many an egg-bound hen was galvanised into frantic productivity for fear of receiving a second dose of Mum's Saturday brew; and if the worm tablets in the orange tin kept our big-boned Kentish sheep from liver fluke, they did the same for us. A passing vet had once pronounced my sister 'weakly', and thereafter she was dosed with blood-mixture and a patent food for feeble calves.

Saturday night's assembly line

At dosing time Dad lit the hurricane lamp and took himself off to the stables. As the youngest, I had my liquorice first; so it seemed downright unjust that on the night of the rebellion mine was the only cup to be emptied. My usually submissive sister stood with lips shut tight, her flushed face turning interesting shades of mauve as she defied the hands that held her nose, after she had declared that death was preferable to liquorice. In the scrimmage the contents of the cup were flung across the table. There was a crack like breaking ice on a frozen pond, and paraffin seeped across the red velvet table-cloth. With a speed that belied her size, Mum snatched the smoking lamp and ran from the kitchen to hurl it on to the wet cobbles in the yard. Firelit shadows crept across the beams of the ceiling, as we children waited in the sort of calm that lies in the eye of a hurricane. The tempest struck. Mum, with copper-stick in hand and retribution in her heart, sent all six of us trembling to our beds.

Justice had been satisfied, the candles taken down, and we lay rattling the knobs on our old brass bedstead. My sister sobbed from injured pride and a sore seat; I lay shivering with fear. Somewhere in our house that awful reptile was probably slithering around in search of her, because she had broken the lamp and set it free.

A more terrifying thought sent me scuttling out of bed, along the dark passage, down the back stairs and into the kitchen, unfamiliar now in the dull light of a hurricane lamp. Dad sat in the high-backed windsor chair and, almost incoherent, I scrambled to the safety of his knee. When words would come I warned him that, although my sister had caused the lamp to be broken, it was Mum who had smashed it. I knew that Dad would not want the snake to eat her, because she was his friend. Only that week I had seen him kiss her in the barn.

Strangely he had no fears. He said the biggest snake in Kent was only half the length of his shepherd's crook, so it would be no match for our cottage-loaf-shaped Mum and could even get a dose of liquorice for its pains. To prove his point he reasoned that the whale-boned armour-plated stays Mum always wore would deter a rhinoceros, much more a slithering little snake.

Mum emerged from the scullery, pink-cheeked, her cotton nightgown buttoned to the neck, carrying her stays. I implored her to wear them night and day. She promised that she would, then held me close to her comforting feather-bolster front.

When I crossed the yard in the morning, I passed the shattered lamp, its wick still coiled up, in a rainbow puddle. It was replaced by a brass affair which gave a flat uninteresting light. The kitchen lost its magic, and its menace, from that day. Medicines we had in plenty, but never again Mum's Saturday brew.

In the barn

Cottage Heirlooms   by Mabel Benson

I hardly know why I so readily accepted the prospect of acting as administrator of the small property of two aged relatives. In a number of other spheres I had learnt that affairs give more trouble writ small than large, but in this one I suppose I had still the lesson to learn. My masculine counterpart would take seriously the bank balances and the Savings Certificates, which for me had little interest and could be left to the professionals. But the furniture, the photographs, the tools were embodied thoughts, solutions to problems and reservoirs of memory. The first thing for me to do was to examine these.

The cottage was an ancient one, originally of two large low-ceiled rooms, one below and one above, with a huge hearth and chimney-stack. But it had been carved up into smaller rooms, and of late years there had been added to the tadpole head of the old cot a thin tail of kitchens, bathroom, wash-houses and tool-rooms, with small apartments above. Beneath the simple orderly appearance of the rooms lurked an unending multiplicity of things. Every cupboard was crammed to the door. Under every bed were closely packed boxes: oak chests ranging from a fine plain one, beautifully made and moving at a touch on brass wheels, to rough ones which were little more than planks nailed together. Compressed into every available space were small household and family effects, of any age from a hundred and fifty or sixty years to five, many of them remnants of legacies and farm sales. They had come from a small Warwickshire dairy farmhouse in the early 1900s, from little country cottages at any time since 1820, from an ironmaster's midland mansion of the sixties or seventies of last century, from a London cabinet-maker's workshop of Regency times, and more lately from a Cotswold arable farm.

I had reason to suppose that my relatives had stern views and preferred austerity. Why then, in a small sitting-room, the plethora of large cushions, and in the bedrooms of deep feather beds? I opened a cushion and found it filled with raw wool. It had all been plucked from the hedges or maybe from the fleeces of sheep that had died by mishap. And the beds were a by-product of fowls and geese consumed by the family (there were bags of feathers hanging on the walls of the outhouses now). It had been a sin and a shame to waste a feather or a strand of wool; hence the combination of strenuous work and soft lying. This spirit of thrift had touched the men of the family, though not so deeply: I remembered the keen Methodist and earnest temperance worker who had gone to live in a house embowered in orchards. He had not been able to bear the sight of heaps of rotting apples and had changed into a maker and connoisseur of cider.

Entering the little sitting-room that had always been used for tea-parties, I reflected that for at least one ancestor life had been more than a long story of work and contrivance. The furniture here was all rosewood and Regency: a small couch with scroll-work ends, and four chairs all of the same general design of subtly curved legs and backs and the same wood, but one with rosettes and another with bows in the decoration of the back, the arms of a third curving so ecstatically as to make almost a circle. The very picture frames belonged: they and the fire-screen on a rod and the pillared mirrors of rosewood and gilt and ebony had all come from the same source. A great-great-aunt of mine had, somewhere about 1835, married an elderly French cabinet-maker working in London. Here in a tiny frame was his card of admission to the Chairmakers' Guild, dated 1829. The legend of this dame was always told in a voice suggesting that she was worldly and selfish, but now I admire the way she kept off her own life the Victorian blight of resignation and excessive domesticity and duty that was falling on the women around her. In her little island of beauty, sustained by her small store in 'the Funds' and 'the Railways', she defied all conventional family demands and unkind village gossip.

In an unused bedroom were two huge old leather trunks with domed lids. They had not been opened for years. Of one the most notable contents were some huge heavy linen cloths whose use I could not imagine. They had been the property of an aunt of my own who had lived to be nearly ninety. Presently an old letter revealed that they were her grandmother's linen sheets, handspun and woven in a Quaker household early in the nine-teenth century or perhaps earlier. They were coarse in the extreme: one would as soon sleep in hessian. Lying with them was a similarly hand-wrought blanket. It had covered the guests in a coaching inn on the road between London and Warwick. Later, when ousted from the beds by the softer, lighter machine-made blankets, it had served to make realistic Bedouin tents for small boys. Now it was honourably entombed as historic.

The contents of the second trunk made a contrast with these stern realities. Here was a huge store of Victorian elegance: for example, some dozens, perhaps scores (I was too entranced to count them), of elaborate tea-table cloths. Some were mere ribbons of linen between broad lace 'insertions', others were of embroidered net, and others again of drawn-thread and Richelieu work. Many were worn out with washing and starching, but some were still worthy of acceptance by a modern bride. Beside these household cloths were ladies' underclothes in a like style: chemises and camisoles with an infinity of fine stitching and lace, both hand-made and machine-made, as well as more homely crochet-work. How bulky the ladies must have looked in all this ample linen!

This contrast in household linen, the heavy-as-lead and the diaphanous, prompts a thought about women. In the nineteenth century leisure and wealthy surroundings came to quite a number, but even for them life was still restricted to the domesticities. They could not, with few exceptions, burst the bonds of the hearth into a broader life, so they went higher and higher into pernickety elegance, sublimating what they must endure. Nor was that true only of the urban and the well-to-do. I can just remember the time when a village girl who could not crochet and do drawn-thread work was hardly a girl at all.

I had to let the books go without survey, but one must look at the manuscripts. Notable among them was an enormous collection of cookery recipes, cut or copied from old magazines, newspapers and travel books. No one could have tried more than a selection of them. Here again was the pathos of the over-domestic life, the repetitive, insufficient relief from narrowness. Somewhat similar in their effect on me at least was an almost equally large collection of pious extracts in verse and prose. Who could possibly have profited by so much aspiration, so much sentiment? In this region one may also put old letters and personal diaries; the latter were short and occasional, written only for lack of the perfect human ear for confidences. An old-fashioned executrix knows the fire to be their correct destination.

Group photographs, however, are public property. One shows a triumphant flower-show committee with the challenge cup recently won; another a festive meeting of, I think, the first and second village classes run by the Workers' Educational Association. A third records a peace-making between a village parson and a Friendly Society of which he had not always approved. In all of them fine faces and heads predominate. Would a group of ourselves come out as well today, I wonder? And if not, is it that our thoughts are not so high or that so many of the sons of these old carpenters, wheelwrights and farmers have gone into the professions? There are also photographs of individual young men and women taken in 1903 and the years round about. How heavy are the young faces! In some more recent photographs of the sons and daughters of these, at the same age, there is great vivacity, and faint lines of laughter are already coming. Hydrogen bombs, I conclude, affect the young less weightily than evangelical piety, unaided ambition and the low prices of farm produce affected their parents.

The kitchens and outhouses provided their share of relics. Most of the utensils there had yielded more to time, but some were brave still. The brass bottle-jack had had its occasional polish, though it must be sixty years at least since it rotated the game or joint before the fire of the kitchen out in the yard of my great-grandmother's house. So had the copper pot, though it must be far longer since, in a poorer household, meat, suet pudding and vegetables were all boiled in it together in one savoury jorum. It was heavy with thick patches but in good condition. (Now again it lives a useful life beside the fire, containing a modern housewife's shop-bought fire-lighters.) From the back of a cupboard came forth the flat beech boards with which brine was squeezed from butter, and the 'hands' with which pound bars and quarter-pound pats were decorated; and the milk-skimmer of tin with its most subtle shallow curve. How recently every mistress of a small farmhouse was a butter-maker!

In an outhouse I found some boards which had a familiar look. When I fitted them together I saw that they were the remnants of a dough-kivver which had gone out of use only about 1900. On shelves in the tool-room were old lanterns and carriage lamps, with remnants of candles still in the sockets. When my father was setting out in his gig on a dark night a child would be called upon to put in new candles, making sure the springs would continue to force them up as they burned away.

Ah, the weight of labour women carried! On Monday a huge family wash, on Tuesday churning and butter-making, and on Wednesday ironing. Thursday was occupied with cleaning one half of the sitting-rooms and bedrooms, and Friday with the others. On Saturday the kitchen and dairies were scrubbed and bread was baked. And what standards the times, the children and the men exacted! Take the ironing: men's collars and cuffs were cold-starched and ironed till they were as stiff as boards, and the children's summer bonnets in my earliest infancy were stiffly frilly with cold starch and hot gophering irons. How thankful I felt as I handled the old utensils that they were used no longer! With what pleasure I contemplated their successors: for example, an early Jones sewing-machine, and an old washing machine so small as to look like a toy! Although made by some unheard-of firm, this still works with a tranquil untiring motion that seems an emblem for all the help that has come to farm women's lives.

COUNTRY PAPERBACKS
FROM DAVID & CHARLES

THE COUNTRYMAN COTTAGE LIFE BOOK
Edited by Fred Archer

FOLKLORE AND CUSTOMS OF RURAL ENGLAND
Margaret Baker

MEMOIRS OF A FEN TIGER
Audrey James

WILD FOX
Roger Burrows